Entertaining and Educating Babies and Toddlers

Expert advice from:
Jo Lafford, NNEB, HPSEB
Lydia Johnsey, BSc, PGCE, BTEC Dip.
Debbie Winder RGN, RM, BSc
Francine Hendrick, MSc, RN, RSCN, RM, RHV

Cover design by Nickey Butler
and Francesca Allen

Americanization: Carrie Armstrong

Entertaining and Educating Babies and Toddlers

Caroline Young

Illustrated by Shelagh McNicholas
and Ruth Russell

Designed by Ruth Russell, Joanne Kirkby
and Laura Hammonds

Edited by Felicity Brooks
and Emma Helbrough

Contents

A wider world (18 – 24 months)

Useful information

Now they are two (2 – 2¹/₂ years)

Introduction

For a newborn baby, the world is an incredible, exciting place – everything is new, just waiting to be discovered. Babies start learning from the moment they are born, and children learn more in their first two years than at any other time in their lives.

They learn from what they see and hear around them. Most importantly, they learn through play. This means that anyone caring for a baby or toddler has a central role in helping them find out about their new world and giving them the chance to play, and learn.

Find out the best activities for babies at different ages.

Get advice on which toys are worth buying.

For little children, the simplest, everyday things are often the most fascinating.

Help toddlers with art ideas and pre-writing skills.

Useful tip

Remember that the ideas suggested for each age group are only guidelines. Experts emphasize that all children are different and develop at their own pace.

Having fun together

This book provides a huge range of simple, inexpensive ideas for activities to do with babies and toddlers up to the age of two-and-a-half. Don't forget that the goal of all the activities is to make finding out about the world fun.

Research shows that babies learn best if you're both enjoying whatever you're doing together, so keep each activity short and leave it until another day if it feels right to do so. Babies can get tired quickly and also pick up on your boredom if you have had enough of bouncing rhymes or peek-a-boo. Try to remember that, for babies, having fun with people who care for them is, quite simply, the best thing in the world.

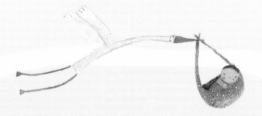

Starting out

The first three months of a baby's life can be a hectic, emotional time for everyone involved, so don't try to do too much, too soon. Although babies are born ready to learn all about the world around them, experts have found that newborns do not enjoy too much noise or activity in these first weeks. Their priorities are to be warm, comfortable, fed and loved.

What can newborn babies do?

Most babies are born knowing how to suck for milk, either from the breast or a bottle.

If babies are held near their mother's breast, or their cheeks are stroked, they'll open their mouths. This is called rooting.

A loud noise or being put down too fast can make newborns spread their arms and legs and grab at the air.

If you put a finger into a newborn's palm, the baby will close its hand tightly around it.

If you hold newborn babies under their armpits, they step with their feet. They soon stop doing this, and don't learn to walk 'for real' until months later.

Getting to know you

The first few days after a baby is born are an unforgettable time. It's easy to feel snowed under with visitors, flowers, diapers… and advice. If you can, just use these early days to get to know your new baby, and let them get to know you and learn about their new world. Give them time to study your face, hear your voice and enjoy being near you.

Experts have discovered that tiny babies can't see very far. They are gradually able to see things clearly that are about as far away as your face if they are in your arms. Things farther away are still blurry at this stage. This limited vision may well protect babies from being too stimulated by everything around them. It also makes sure they concentrate on getting to know the person caring for them. You'll notice they do turn toward a light, such as a lamp.

Being close to someone who cares for them is what newborns find most reassuring.

Newborn babies usually find faces fascinating. Let them spend some time getting to know yours.

Close to you

For newborns, being near someone who cares for them is usually what makes them happiest. Take the opportunity to let them be close to you whenever you can. Nothing awful will happen if you leave the dirty dishes for another half an hour, so allow yourself time to help a newborn relax, and get used to the world they have so recently arrived in. Of course, babies have to spend time in their strollers or bassinets, but they need the reassuring comfort of closeness, too.

After a feeding, give babies time to relax and enjoy the comfort of just being with you.

Face to face

Spend some time letting a baby study your face. Starting at around three weeks, they can see it clearly and if you smile at them, within weeks they'll probably smile back. Some experts believe even very young babies can tell the difference between sad and happy facial expressions.

Sound sensitivity

Babies are very sensitive to sound, and hear well. Try not to make loud noises, such as slamming a door, near newborns, as you could frighten them. Keep the room that they sleep in quiet and calm if you can, without too many distractions. Research shows that some babies relax when they hear rhythmical background noises, such as vacuum cleaners or hair dryers. They might remember having heard these everyday sounds when they were in the womb.

Newborn babies know their mother's voice first, but soon recognize and start to respond to the voices of other 'important' people by becoming still when they speak, or by turning toward them.

Talking to even the tiniest of babies can help them begin to learn the sounds and rhythms of everyday speech. Many babies enjoy just hearing people talk around them – they really don't mind what's being said. Let them spend time just listening to the daily goings-on in your home: after the soft noises in the womb, they're not used to complete silence.

Even newborn babies enjoy hearing you speak.

Talk to a tiny baby as much as you can, using a soft, gentle tone.

A baby's bed needs to be comfortable, safe — and interesting.

Crib entertainment

Babies spend a lot of their time in bed – be it a crib, Moses basket or bassinet. Much of the time, they are sleeping, so it is important that their bed is comfortable and safe. It's fine for them to spend some time awake in bed, too, if they are happy to do so. Tiny babies can't move around and see interesting things, so things need to be brought to them. Babies are far happier to spend some time awake in their cribs if it is an interesting place to be.

First mobiles

Health professionals advise always putting babies on their backs to sleep, which means there's plenty of opportunity for them to look at something hanging down above them, such as a mobile. By eight weeks, most babies' vision will have improved enough for them to be able to see a mobile hanging from the ceiling. By about three months old, they can see most things, even at some distance.

There are many kinds of mobiles available, of varying design and expense. Some clip onto the crib, others play music, spin around, or even flash lights on the ceiling. Studies show that babies like looking at curved lines more than straight ones, and are more interested in 3-D objects than flat ones, so choose a mobile that you feel will be interesting. Try to see it from a baby's point of view, when you are buying one.

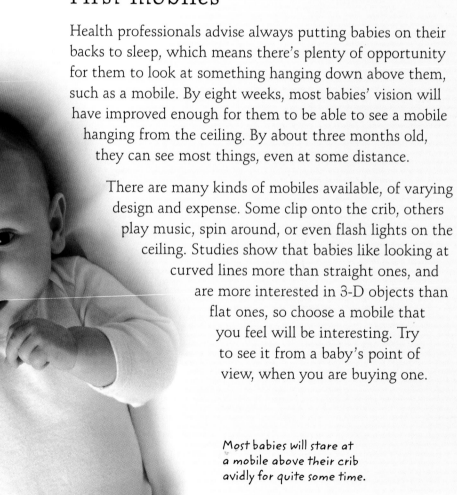

Most babies will stare at a mobile above their crib avidly for quite some time.

Mobiles and crib books

Babies love looking at a variety of different colors and textures. Some mobiles have detachable toys that can be replaced with other toys for variety. 'Everyday' items will also fascinate babies. They may enjoy seeing a feather, tinsel or party streamer that you hold for them. (Be sure not to leave babies unsupervised with these items.)

Within three months, babies can turn to the right and left in their cribs. Drawings and books with simple patterns (often called crib or stroller books) give them something to look at. Research shows babies are more attracted by pictures with strong color contrasts in them.

Feather

Party decoration

Wallpaper strip

Babies are often so excited to see something new that they will wiggle and kick.

1. Try drawing a spiral and some shapes, or a checkered pattern on white cardboard with a dark, non-toxic marker.

2. Safely attach the picture to the inside of the crib, where the baby can see it easily. Change the picture if the baby seems bored with it.

Babies alone

However many interesting things you provide, they'll only entertain a baby for a short time. Babies at this stage are just too small to play alone for long. If they're fed, dry and tired, it's safe to leave them to cry for a while, but if they keep crying, it's better to see what they need. Some babies do cry more than others, and take longer to settle, and experts often can't explain exactly why. It may help to remind yourself that a baby can only tell you they're unhappy by crying. If you can, try to keep calm, and remember that this common phase will pass.

Safety point

Make sure that toys placed in or near a baby's bed are securely attached and well out of their grasp at this age.

• Take your diaper bag, spare baby clothes, and bottles (if you use them) whenever you go out.

• Remember to take a sunshade or a rain cover for your stroller, in case you need them.

• It's tricky to hold an umbrella while pushing a stroller, so it might be a good idea to wear a coat with a hood.

Venturing out

It's inevitable that, for the first few weeks after a baby arrives, life will be very busy for everyone involved in this new, full-time job. It can seem difficult to do anything except feed, wash clothes and change diapers. Planning to go out with the baby can seem a tall order, but is a good idea for both of you.

Try to set out after a feeding and diaper change, if possible.

With a little advance planning and good timing, outings don't have to be stressful. Don't set off if the baby needs a diaper change, or may need to be fed soon, for example. Just try to have a change of scene, and some fresh air. Even the simplest of outings helps break up the day for someone caring for a new baby.

Experiencing the world

Babies can't move themselves around at this stage, but many enjoy the sensation of movement, such as being carried in a sling or riding in a stroller or car. Although they need to lie flat, or almost flat, they can still see lights, the sky and trees above, and people's faces. Research shows it's also important for babies to be talked to and to be able to see who's talking. It may feel strange at first, but 'telling' them about the things that you pass will make the experience much richer for them.

A short visit to a local park provides many new sensations for a tiny baby.

Meeting other people

If you know anyone else with a new baby, try getting together to chat about how things are going. It can be very reassuring for you to meet other people going through these early weeks, so it's really worth the effort. Tiny babies will not 'play' with each other yet, but may enjoy hearing and seeing each other. Recent research showed that even very young babies are aware of each other and may benefit from being together in some way.

Strangers may want a peek at a tiny baby. This may seem nosy, but babies often love seeing new faces.

Babies in cars

Most babies travel in a car within days of being born and are often calmed by its motion. Perhaps it reminds them of the cushioned movement they felt inside the womb. Whatever the reason, a drive may quieten crying newborns, and even long journeys are often not a problem, as they are usually soothed to sleep.

When you buy a car seat, don't be afraid to ask for clear instructions on how to use it. Often your local hospitals and safety officials can help you install the seat in your car.

Safety points

If you're taking a baby in a car, they are never safe in your arms or on your lap. They must be securely strapped in a baby car seat facing the rear of the car.

Never place a car seat on the front passenger seat with an air bag — it can injure or even kill a baby.

Small steps

In the last few weeks, your life will have changed enormously. Things that you used to take for granted, such as a quick trip to the store, or meeting friends, are not quite as simple with a tiny baby, and do take more time. As with any big change, it may take a while to get used to. Take things slowly, don't expect too much of yourself, and try to accept that, right now, things feel very different.

Useful tip

If you can't go out, ask friends to come to you. Most will love taking care of a new baby while you take a bath or make you both some lunch.

Keeping babies busy

When you are taking care of a baby, there are usually more things that need to be done at home, but less time to do them in. Keeping on top of things can be stressful, especially if the baby only seems happy when you are around. Some of the ideas here may help, though.

Getting chores done

If you have outdoor chores to do, you can make things easier by taking a baby outside, either in a stroller, car seat or bouncy chair. Put this somewhere where the baby can see and hear you, make sure they are strapped in safely, and keep looking at them and chatting as you do things. Don't forget to keep them warm, shaded from the sun and protected from insects and cats, with a net, too.

If a baby is not happy in a bouncy chair, stroller or car seat, you could try putting them in a sling. Using a sling means the baby can be near you, hear and smell you, but you don't have to stay in one place. Keep checking that the baby is not too heavy for the sling. By three months old some are, which means that carrying them could hurt your back.

Babies may be happy watching you from a car seat...

...or while bouncing in a bouncy chair, as long as you keep chatting with them.

A sling leaves your hands free, but you need to protect the baby's head. This kind is not suitable for newborns as they need one with a head support.

Safety point

Most bouncy chairs are safe from a few weeks after birth, some even sooner. Never use them on a slippery or unstable surface. On the floor is best.

Changing-time fun

Changing the baby's diaper is a job you will have to do thousands of times in the months ahead. If you make it as enjoyable as you can for both of you, the baby may gain more from the experience than just a clean, dry bottom. Here are some tips to keep things fun.

• Keep chatting as you change a diaper. The baby won't understand, but will be listening and learning.

• Most babies enjoy being diaperless for a while, in a warm room. Let them lie on a towel on the floor.

• Some babies really hate being changed. Try tickling their toes gently to distract them from crying.

• Kiss the baby's tummy or blow a raspberry softly on it. It is usually covered up, and so gets touched less.

Diaper changing is a good time for some one-to-one interaction.

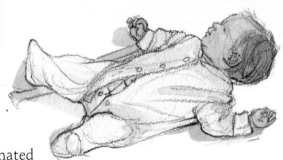

Faces and mirrors

Babies at this stage seem programmed to be fascinated with faces – especially their own – and recent research suggests that there may be a special part of their brains that recognizes faces. At first, they focus just on the central panel down the middle of a face, especially the mouth. As the weeks pass, they begin to see the individual features, but it may take up to a year for a baby to recognize themselves. Learning to 'read' facial expressions is an important skill for a baby to acquire and a mirror is ideal for this, as it lets them study their own face, not just yours. Below are some suggestions for ways to use mirrors.

Useful tip
Don't be alarmed if a baby cries at unfamiliar people's faces. It's nothing personal, just a common baby response.

1. Hold the baby facing the mirror and say, 'Look! there's Jack' (or whatever the baby's name is). Then move the baby away, saying, 'Where did he go?'

2. Now hold the baby facing backward over your shoulder, so they can see their face close-up. Most will be mesmerized by the little face looking back at them.

3. Try wedging a non-breakable toy mirror down one side of a stroller. Babies will be able to look at it and look away when they want to.

• Babies respond to music their mother listened to when she was pregnant, such as a TV theme.

• Crying babies are often soothed by soft, calm music and can be upset or startled by loud music.

• Babies prefer some songs over others and quickly start to recognize their favorites.

• The more you sing a familiar song, the better. Babies learn by things being repeated over and over.

Sound, music and songs

From the moment they leave the safe, muffled environment of the womb, babies are surrounded by all kinds of new sounds. They still need some quiet times, of course – but they learn little from total silence. Introducing a baby to sounds, music and songs can be enjoyable for both of you.

Music and mood

Even tiny babies seem to enjoy music, and studies show that it can really affect their mood. It helps them learn about rhythm, too, which helps with speech development. Many babies like dancing in their caregiver's arms. Holding the baby securely, try dancing gently to some music. Being close to you, sharing your enjoyment and hearing new sounds is a real pleasure for them.

You can show a baby how much you are enjoying the music by the expression on your face, or by gently tapping out the beat.

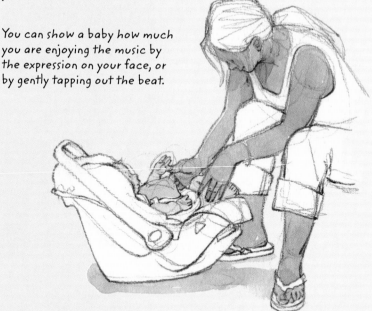

Try dancing gently to some music, holding the baby in your arms. Make sure to support the baby's head.

It's fine to let babies listen to lots of different kinds of music. Recent research shows that many babies respond to classical music in the same way they do to hearing people speak: they listen intently to its flow and rhythm. Some experts believe that listening to classical music can help children develop better in several areas of learning.

Singing songs

Even if you feel your singing is terrible, your baby will be your biggest fan. There are some suggestions for songs and rhymes you could sing on pages 114–117. If you prefer, you can buy or download recordings of songs or music for babies. Playing lullabies at bedtime can be an especially good idea, as babies often link those songs with 'sleep time'.

Singing is a tried and tested way of soothing a fretful baby.

What's that noise?

Newborn babies can hear all kinds of sounds, but don't know where they come from. Beginning at about four weeks old, many begin to turn their eyes or head toward the source of a sound to try to find this out. To help them, try some of the baby toys available that rattle, ring, squeak and rustle. Many baby books also have pages that make an interesting noise if you squeeze or press them. Remember always to give a baby plenty of time, and lots of chances, to connect the noise with the thing that is making it.

Put some coins or dried beans in a plastic container and securely replace the lid. Shake the container gently to make it rattle.

Involve babies in the comings and goings of your home by making sure there's plenty for them to listen to whenever they are awake.

Gently shake a rattle toy to one side of the baby's head...

...the baby may turn their eyes or head toward the sound.

When you sing, tap out the rhythm on the soles of your baby's feet. This lets them 'feel' the tune.

Say a baby's name often. They quickly learn that that 'sound' is special to them and may turn toward you or smile.

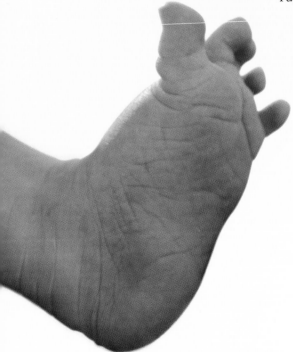

Give babies time to move
their arms and legs freely,
and to explore their
fingers and toes.

Safety point

It is never safe to
leave a baby on a blanket
where you cannot see them,
either inside or outside.

Fists and feet

At first, babies mainly use their senses of sight, smell and hearing to find out about things. As the weeks pass, they begin to reach out for toys, and swipe at things. Toward the end of their first three months, they begin to move their arms and legs much more deliberately. They are gradually learning how the different parts of their body move, and what happens when they move them.

Both of you will probably enjoy songs and rhymes that involve you gently touching or tickling the baby's fingers and toes. 'Round and round the garden' and 'This little piggy' are good ones to try. (Find the words and actions on page 116.) Remember that the tone of your voice, and how enthusiastic you sound are important to a baby's enjoyment. The more you repeat the rhymes, the more the baby begins to predict when the tickle or hug will come. You may get bored with the rhymes, but, for babies, repetition is essential.

Blanket time

Babies cannot build on their new movement skills if they are always in their crib or strapped into a chair or stroller. Try letting a baby lie on a blanket or on a soft, clean rug on the floor, where their arms and legs can move around completely freely. It's good for their toes to have some sock-free time, too. Most babies start watching their own hands and then reaching for their toes around three months old.

Babies have
very sensitive
fingers and toes.

18

Reaching out

Babies are naturally curious, but they are more likely to stretch out and reach for something if they really want to touch it. As a baby nears three months, you could try a baby gym. These are padded play centers with hanging toys for babies to bat and kick. There are plenty to choose from with colors and shapes that will interest a baby at this stage.

Babies love gripping a finger or having their palms gently tickled.

Everyday objects

Babies may also like kicking and reaching for a few 'everyday' objects such as the ones suggested below. Make sure that all items are safe for babies (larger than 2 inches in diameter with no sharp points) and tied securely on short strings.

• A clean sock, filled with scrunched-up paper. This will be soft to kick and it will make a good noise.

• Tie up some plastic cooking spoons or plastic cookie cutters with string. They will rattle when swiped.

• Pompom balls will move easily when kicked or swiped. Make sure these are larger than 2 inches in diameter.

• If you hang a rattle from your gym, your baby begins to learn that it makes a noise when it moves.

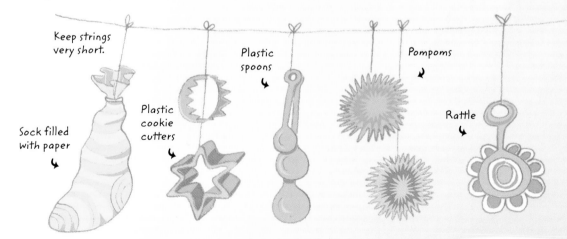

Keep strings very short.

Plastic spoons

Pompoms

Plastic cookie cutters

Sock filled with paper

Rattle

Some commercial baby gyms are designed so that a baby can lie under them on the floor. Some have soft surfaces for the baby to lie on. Others have toys you can take off and change for variety. Whichever you choose, remember to take the gym away if a baby seems bored or frustrated, as they can't move away for a break without help.

Safety point
Never leave toys tied onto or nearby beds or play areas. Make sure your baby is supervised with toys and baby gyms. Remove these from the sleeping area when not in use.

1. Make sure the water is warm, not hot. Test it by dipping your elbow in first; the water should not feel hot on the skin of your elbow.

2. Gently lower the baby in, supporting their head with one arm behind the body and holding the shoulder. Keep talking as you do this.

3. Use your free hand to swoosh a wave of water up over the baby's body. If this goes well, try trickling water on their tummy.

Bathtime

For a baby, bathtime is not about getting clean; it's a play session in water and a chance to feel close to the person bathing them. It also soon becomes part of their understanding of a daily routine, so the sound of the water running may produce excited kicking, as the baby knows it's bathtime. Make sure you have everything ready before you start, so you can both relax and enjoy it.

If you smile and talk softly as you bathe a baby, you will reassure them that all is well.

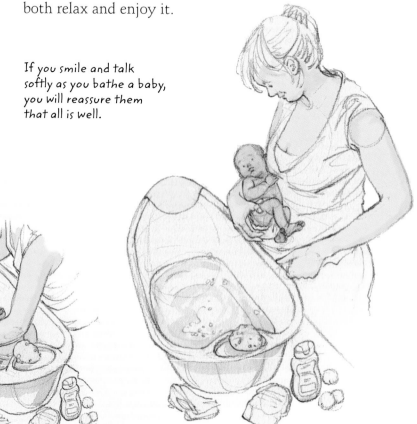

A bath in warm water soothes most babies, whatever the time of day.

Safety point

Babies can drown in a small amount of water very quickly. **Never** leave them alone in the bathtub, even for a moment.

Just for fun

Although bathtime can form part of your daily routine, it can be fun to let a baby enjoy splashing in a bath at other times as well. Fretful babies often calm down in a warm bath too. Let the baby kick and splash freely. They'll enjoy it all the more if you respond enthusiastically. They're learning that being in water is fun.

Bathing together

Sharing a bath with a baby can be enjoyable for both of you, but you need to be organized and have another adult nearby to help. Make sure that the water temperature suits the baby (about 90–95°F), which may mean it's a little cool for you. A baby bath thermometer might be worth buying to check. Ask the other adult to hand the baby to you once you are in the bathtub, and take them from you before you get out.

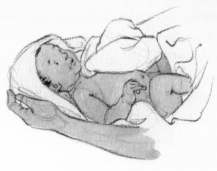

Babies need to be dried quickly once they're out of the water, so have a towel ready.

Bath toys

Providing toys that a baby only sees in the bathtub makes the event more special. They can be a useful distraction, too, if a baby is tired or fussy. There are many bath books and toys available; boats and bobbing ducks are usually popular. You could try hiding a toy in the water and then playing 'peekaboo'. You may be rewarded with chuckles each time the toy bobs up.

Make gentle stroking movements with the towel to dry the baby's delicate skin.

After-bath massage

Even tiny babies usually enjoy being gently massaged, but some don't like their tummies being rubbed. If a baby seems unhappy in any way when you follow the steps below, just leave it for another day.

1. Make sure the room is warm. Put the baby on a dry towel on the changing table, or on the floor.

2. Put a few drops of baby oil on one hand. (Don't use nut oil or anything perfumed.) Rub hands together.

3. Stroke down the baby's legs and arms. Turn the baby over and massage the back with smooth strokes.

4. Talking softly will help babies to relax. Wrap them in the towel to warm up before you dress them.

Time to touch

Between three and six months, most babies
find out how to reach, touch and hold on to things
around them. They begin to move more, too, and
will become more vocal. The ideas in this section
are designed to suit babies at this stage, but
remember every baby develops at a different pace,
so always be guided by what your baby enjoys
when you choose activities.

How will my baby change?

During these months, most babies learn to hold their heads
up when they want to look at something interesting.

They start to make a lot of sounds known as
'babbling'. These are the beginnings of speech.

They learn how to use their hands to
hold, and even pick up, objects.

They learn to roll over and move across the floor, and
can stand if you hold them around the chest.

Toys and teeth

During these months, most babies want to touch things or put them into their mouths. Learning how to touch and then hold a toy held in front of them is a tricky skill to master and takes a lot of practice to get right. The main thing you need to help a baby at this stage is patience.

Touching and mouthing

Learning to touch and hold is hard work, and babies get tired and frustrated quickly. They will fail in their efforts many times, but bear with them. Make it more interesting by holding up different toys for them to reach for. It's a good idea to wash toys in hot, soapy water regularly, as babies will put them into their mouths. This is called 'mouthing' and they do it to find out about things as the nerve endings in their mouths are extremely sensitive.

Teething trouble

By six months old, many babies have some tiny teeth. 'Teething' babies can cry more, droul or have a red, sore bottom. They also tend to put absolutely everything into their mouths, so don't leave anything around that isn't safe.

Teething babies often have red cheeks and want to suck on anything they can reach.

1. Hold a small toy, such as a rattle, in front of the baby. Keep it still while the baby tries to move a hand toward it.

2. When the baby touches the toy, gently put it in their palm. They may drop it, or try to tighten their fingers around it.

3. Many babies put the toy straight into their mouths. Let them suck and lick it before you take it away.

Safety point

Never let babies hold something small that could choke them. Ensure objects they play with are bigger than their mouths.

• Baby books are designed to be simple and repetitive, which most babies respond to and enjoy.

• Books offer a taste of how words and pictures work together.

• Hearing familiar words read again and again helps babies learn what they mean and how to say them.

• Books feed a child's growing imagination, providing a source of pleasure that can last a lifetime.

Beginning with books

It's never too early to introduce babies to books. Long before they can read a word or turn a page, research shows that babies benefit in several ways from looking at books with an adult, or with an older child. Preschool children who regularly spend time 'reading' with an adult are more likely to develop good spoken language skills, so reading aloud to babies is really worthwhile.

Choosing books

Looking at a book with a baby is a good chance to spend some time with them, without any distractions. It also helps them begin to get to know how books 'work' and how pages can be turned. There is a huge variety of books available for babies. If you feel daunted, try borrowing a selection from a library before buying any, to see which ones go over well. The tips on these two pages may also help you choose some baby books.

Books for babies must be safe for them to handle. This means they will probably be made of board, cloth or vinyl.

Studies show that books with big pictures of familiar things are ideal. Babies start to recognize things they see every day.

Even small babies enjoy cuddling up with a good book.

What do I do?

Experts believe that young children who see people around them enjoying reading books, papers or magazines find it easier to learn how to read themselves. From the beginning, try to make the time you look at books together fun and relaxing for both of you.

1. Choose a good baby book and a time when the baby is not tired or hungry. Sit somewhere comfortable with the baby in your lap, so they can see and touch the pages.

2. Say the name of the object on each page or try counting things, pointing to them as you speak. Is there a noise that goes with the picture, too?

3. Don't make the experience formal or rush through the pages. If the baby wants to grab the book and suck it, let them. If they turn away, they might have had enough.

4. Talk about the pictures if you can. 'This car is red,' will be fascinating to a baby if you make it sound so. Repeat the words several times.

If you feel awkward 'talking' to a baby, you may find that having a book to look at together can make it easier.

Again and again and...

Frankly, looking at the same, very simple, picture books day after day can be pretty boring for you. If you can, try to remember that babies love hearing a familiar book, song or rhyme countless times. They feel reassured that everything in it remains the same. Eventually, a baby will have enough of a favorite book and move on to a new one – and there's a huge choice for both of you...

Look for cloth books with rattling, squishy and squeaky pages and bright pictures.

Board books with textured patches for little fingers to feel are often popular.

Suitable for a baby from birth, 'accordion' books can be attached to crib bars or tucked inside a bassinet.

Time to sit up

Babies at this stage begin trying to sit upright. The main reason for this is so they can see more – but it's hard work. Some strain to lift their heads when they're on their backs, for instance. Encourage them by holding their hands and pulling them gently. This strengthens their muscles, and their confidence.

As a baby's awareness of what's around them grows, they'll want to see more.

Muscle power

Babies need a lot of strength, muscle control and balance to sit up on their own. They need to learn how to lift their heads first of all, for which they need strong back and neck muscles. At this stage babies start strengthening these muscles by trying to lift their heads while lying on their tummies.

If they get frustrated, hold their hands and very gently lift them to a sitting position.

Starting at about four months, most babies' head and neck muscles strengthen rapidly.

They learn to raise and hold their heads up when lying on their tummies, but it's very tiring for them.

Useful tip

Try holding up a plastic toy mirror in front of a baby when they're lying on their tummy, so they can peek at themselves when their head is raised.

You can encourage a baby by lying down to face them. They will copy you and feel rewarded for their efforts. When the baby lifts their head, lift yours, smile and say 'Boo!'. Older siblings might enjoy doing this activity, as babies usually laugh heartily when greeted with another face. Make sure the game stops if a baby is tired, though.

Which toys?

As babies master the skill of sitting upright, try building a safe play area for them on the floor. Build a 'support wall' of cushions and pillows behind the baby and spread out a few toys or safe, everyday objects at their feet. Babies at this stage can only pick up and give their attention to one object at a time. Studies show that they can get confused if presented with too many. Remember that if the toys roll away, the baby can't get them back, so choose things that don't roll or be there to roll them back.

Babies of this age are mainly interested in what they can do with things they play with. If you give them two or three different playthings, they will suck, touch, explore and learn from them, in their own way.

A 'wall' of cushions on the floor helps a baby sit upright.

Safety point

Never leave a propped up baby alone. They may fall or slip down and not be able to breathe.

Activity centers

Activity centers are popular with most babies starting at around five months and are ideal toys for babies who are just sitting up. They have parts that move, feel interesting, or make noises, and each is specifically designed for babies to enjoy looking at and exploring. You may be able to borrow an activity center from a friend, but this is one toy that may be worth buying.

An activity center provides plenty for a sitting baby to explore.

A big blanket spread out on the floor makes a safe play area, but keep an eye on the baby at all times.

Bouncing babies

Babies at this stage can't crawl or walk, but most love to roll, kick and bounce. These activities strengthen their muscles, ready for when they'll move on their own. It's easy to provide ways for babies to stretch and move, but you need to judge if they're ready for them. Some find it hard to hold their heads up for long, for example, and get tired quickly. Go at the baby's own pace and stop if the activity is no longer fun.

Most babies enjoy being free to move in a large, safe space, so move anything that could get in the way and spread a blanket out on the floor. If you put some toys out, or lie down near the baby, they'll want to reach out even more.

Bouncing, stretching and other active play helps to build a baby's muscle strength.

Nursery rhymes

Some nursery rhymes, action rhymes and songs are ideal for babies who enjoy bouncing. Two of the best are 'Horsey, horsey' and 'This is the way the ladies ride', but you'll find a selection on pages 114–117. Research shows that, even at this stage, babies begin to recognize rhymes that you sing to them regularly. They gradually learn to 'predict' the part where they get lifted into the air or gently bounced, with a smile of recognition or with excited eyes.

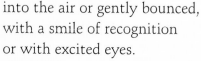

Useful tip
Choose the time for bouncing games carefully. Don't try them with a tired baby or one who has a tummy full of milk for instance.

Rhymes and songs that involve a little gentle tickling and bouncing may go over well.

Leg stretches

Many babies enjoy stretching their legs. Here are two ways of letting them stretch and flex their leg muscles while they are having fun with you. If you are feeling brave, you could put a towel over your knees and on the floor and let the baby enjoy the feeling of doing these leg-stretching activities without wearing a diaper.

One foot on each knee

Gentle cycling movements

Try just letting a baby stand on your knees while you hold their waist or chest. They may bounce happily for a few minutes, but you'll need to help them sit down again.

You can stretch a baby's legs by moving them in gentle 'cycling' movements when the baby is on the floor or changing table. Let the baby push their legs against your hands.

Bouncing alone

By this stage, most babies discover that if they bounce, their bouncy chair bounces too. This can give pleasure – and exercise – but always make sure that the straps are fastened securely at all times.

If you can buy a door bouncer, many babies who are nearing six months old enjoy kicking and bouncing in one. Babies have to be able to hold their heads up really well and be almost able to sit before you try them in a bouncer, though. Don't leave a baby in there for long; bouncers provide such a good work-out that they are very tiring.

It takes concentration and determination for babies to learn to use their legs and it can be very tiring.

Safety point

Remember to follow the manufacturer's instructions on size and weight limitations for bouncers.

On the move

During the second six months of their lives, babies learn to sit up on their own, to crawl, and may start trying to walk. Many will try to say their first 'words' and enjoy a variety of new foods. Every child reaches these milestones at their own pace, which can differ a lot. Remember that if you offer babies a range of chances to learn and develop, they will do so. This is also a good time to start babyproofing your home.

How will my baby change?

After six months, most babies are ready to try solid foods. By 12 months they can eat a wide variety of foods, cut small.

Babies become much better at using their hands and learning how things fit together and come apart.

Babies' individual personalities begin to emerge much more. They can get frustrated and show anger.

Most babies learn to crawl at about nine months. They may climb and move so quickly it will surprise you.

Few babies walk before they are one, but many start trying to take a few wobbly steps if they hold your hand.

Fun with food

Health professionals agree that the only food most babies need until they are six months old is breast or formula milk. Babies should be introduced to solid food gradually, over the following months. The ideas on the right will help you make a baby's early experiences of food and eating enjoyable and successful. Some babies find taking food from a spoon tricky at first. They need practice to get used to it. After all, it's completely different from a nipple or bottle, and feels strange in their mouths.

Studies show that introducing a wide variety of tastes and textures can help prevent children from being fussy eaters later. As you introduce new kinds, you may find the baby prefers food that looks interesting. Spotting food we eat in books or magazines can reinforce the idea that 'food is good'.

• If spoonfuls of food are spat straight out, this is very normal. Just keep trying... and keep calm.

• Reward a spoonful successfully swallowed with lots of smiles and praise. Try to keep things positive.

• When babies keep their mouths clamped shut, try opening your mouth. If they copy you, pop the spoon in.

• Giving a baby a spoon to play with while you feed them with another can make things easier.

Coping with mess

Babies are responsive to the mood of their caregivers. Hard as it can be, try not to get upset if they make a mess or don't eat much. Your priorities are to get them to enjoy eating and to keep mealtimes as stress-free as you possibly can.

Babies need lots of encouragement to start eating food from a spoon.

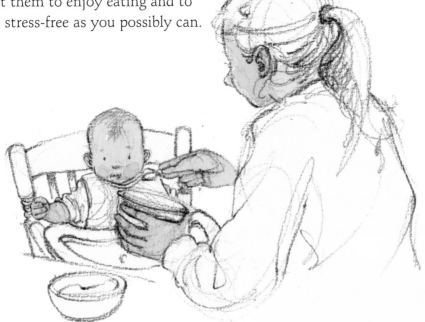

Baby talk

Babies are learning how to talk long before they say anything. For the first months of their lives, they listen to what people say around them, filing away these sounds and rhythms until the day they are ready to say a recognizable word. This usually starts to happen when a baby is just over a year old. There are lots of simple ways of encouraging babies to talk.

The more you respond to a baby's babbling with smiles, hugs or words, the more they'll want to ' talk.'

Babies begin to learn how conversations work by listening to yours.

• Babies who are spoken to often have a much bigger vocabulary of words they can say by the time they are two.

• Research shows that children who are good talkers and listeners are more likely to become good readers and writers.

• Songs, nursery rhymes, action rhymes and baby books all help babies learn to talk. Find out more about using books with babies on pages 24–25.

Having a chat

Babies all over the world say the same sounds first. These are usually 'aaah' or 'oooh' noises. As weeks pass, most add 'm' and 'p' and 'b' to make noises like 'maaa' and 'paaa'. When they begin to say several of these together, it is called babbling. Babies will babble even if nobody responds, but if you 'answer' them, they'll try to form more, new sounds.

Babies who listen to lots of talking learn that people leave gaps for other people to talk in during a conversation. Babies as young as three months old will wait for a response after they have 'said' something. To help them learn, wait until they've finished babbling, then answer in some way. If they babble again, pause and then respond again.

What shall I say?

The idea of talking to babies sounds simple enough, but it can feel strange to talk to someone who is not going to talk back to you. Babies at this stage enjoy hearing things repeatedly, as it helps them to learn. Games that involve hiding something and then producing it again are a good way of using the same speech patterns again and again. Babies will probably also find it fun if you copy the sounds they make. On the right are some other ideas to try.

Little learners

Amazingly, all babies are born with the capacity to learn all the basic sounds in all the world's languages. By the time they are one, they have lost this ability and focus on the language (or languages) spoken most around them. If parents or caregivers speak different languages, experts recommend that each person speaks only their mother tongue to and around the baby, even if it's not the main language the child will need when they go to school.

• Describe everyday actions. Phrases like 'Time to change your diaper' are things you will say many, many times, but repetition is fine.

• You don't need to over-simplify every word you say, but it's helpful to say important, everyday words such as 'spoon' or 'cup' clearly.

• Let the baby see your mouth as you speak. If you hold them up in front of a mirror and talk, they may try to copy what your mouth does.

• Giving the baby a running commentary on daily life may feel a little over the top, but talking about some of the things you both see and do is fun.

Let babies watch, and even touch, your mouth as you talk to them.

Useful tip

Making eye contact with a baby and sounding enthusiastic about what they say encourages them to talk more.

Making music

Most babies at this stage love being bounced on your knees or slid down your legs as you enjoy songs and rhymes together. They may accompany music by bashing toys on highchair trays, or making joyful noises. Many also love jiggling their bodies in time to a beat. Latest research shows that listening to music is one of the best ways for babies and toddlers to learn about rhythm, movement and sound.

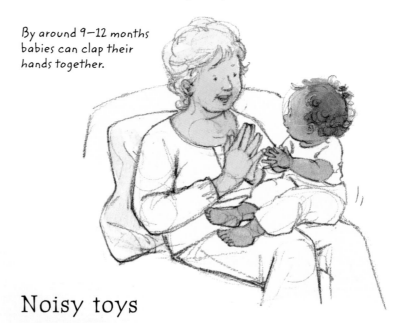

By around 9–12 months babies can clap their hands together.

Baby like toys that make good clacking noises.

Noisy toys

There are plenty of different musical toys available for this age group, but they may not be any more fun for a baby than simple things that make a noise. You could try a music session with some homemade instruments, such as the ones suggested below.

Toys that clink, jingle or squeak are always popular.

• Pans, cans or buckets become drums when hit with a spoon. This helps babies learn about cause and effect; 'when they hit it, it makes a noise'.

• Put some dried beans inside a plastic soda or water bottle with the lid securely screwed on and let the baby listen to the sounds when it tilts.

• Put some large dried pasta in a plastic container with a lid that can be securely attached to make a rattle. Make sure it's strong enough to survive squeezing and sucking.

• Show the baby how to hold two plastic cups and clack them together to make a horsey clip-clop sound.

Music machines

CD players or tape recorders designed for young children can be a good buy for several reasons. Babies enjoy listening to 'their' music, and learning how to use the chunky buttons. Making the music stop and start when they press them often becomes a game.

Show a baby how to press the 'start' button on the music player.

Encourage babies to jiggle, 'sing along' or shake a rattle in time to the music.

• Songs with sounds like a train's 'toot' or duck's 'quack' are a fun way of helping babies listen to and copy sounds.

• Joining a baby music group is a sociable experience for you both and a good way to learn some new songs, too.

• Action rhymes help babies' memories. They need to remember when to clap 'pat-a-cake' or 'row the boat' as you sing.

• If you tap out the beat of the words of songs, you may help a baby remember the words, and, later, use them in speech.

Question and answer

Hearing and making sounds of any kind helps babies learn to recognize sounds and patterns in speech. You can help them develop the listening skills they will need as they learn to talk by having a musical 'conversation' with them. Give the baby a rattle, and hold one yourself. Shake yours, and see if the baby shakes theirs in reply. This activity is ideal for older siblings to try, as they often like to feel they are 'teaching' the baby something.

Dancing

Most babies at this age are eager to stand, and this makes dancing together an ideal activity. They'll bounce happily if you hold their hands. The choice of music is up to you. Try movements, such as stomping your feet in time to the music. Most babies try to copy what you do, which helps their coordination.

Babies may enjoy the rhythm if you sit them on your lap and stomp your feet in time to the music.

Learning to crawl

Babies at this stage are very curious and becoming more mobile. This means they may reach things that were out of bounds before, so safety is particularly important now. On these pages, you will find some safe, fun ideas for beginner crawlers.

Rollers and shufflers

Babies learn to crawl at different times, and in different ways. Some move like crabs, others shuffle on their bottoms; some don't really crawl at all, but roll or slither. The main objective of all their efforts is to explore their environment, but it can be a frustrating process for many babies. Experts believe that babies need to learn several skills to crawl and move their bodies around. Their brain 'sees' their arms and legs and sends messages to their limbs to tell them how to move. It can take many attempts before both brain and limbs remember what to do.

At first babies are happy just to look at things from a sitting position...

Gradually, they realize that there may be more interesting things over there.

Babies have to put in a huge amount of effort to get their body to do what they want it to.

Useful tip

Babies can't learn to crawl if they're in a playpen, highchair or stroller too much of the time. They need 'free' time on a floor, but make sure you never leave them unattended.

If a baby gets really frustrated with not being able to move, try placing a familiar toy a little in front of them to encourage them. If you sit on the floor ahead of them, they will probably try as hard as they can to reach you.

Ready, set... crawl!

The only thing a baby needs to learn to crawl is the floor or the ground. Long pants will protect their knees, but be prepared for them to get grubby. There's no need to move all your furniture for babies, but make sure there is nothing dangerous around, and never leave babies unsupervised.

Reward them with smiles and give them a cuddle if they get fed up. Some babies don't like being on their tummies for long, and will cry. As with most activities suggested in this book, babies like nothing better than you doing it too, so here are some ways of encouraging new crawlers:

Dress a baby who is learning to crawl in thick pants or tights.

Beginner crawlers tire quickly from all their efforts.

- Try getting down on your hands and knees and crawling next to the baby in a mini race.

- You may find that a baby will follow you around the room if you crawl ahead of them.

- Let babies crawl on dry grass (but check for hazards first). They may find it easier and more interesting.

Safe and entertained

While a baby's curiosity and growing mobility is wonderful, it is not always very convenient, or at all safe, for them to empty out all your kitchen cabinets or crawl around your feet while you are cooking. Here are some ways of keeping a baby at this busy stage both safe and entertained at home:

Safety point
Always make sure there's no dog mess, broken glass, lawn chemicals or other hazards on the ground before you let a baby crawl around outside.

Try letting babies play with safe things from just one cabinet. Put child-resistant locks on the others.

Put the baby in a playpen while you are cooking or on the phone. Keep things to play with in it.

You can purchase toys that suction on, or that can be safely attached to highchairs.

Early explorers

Crawling babies are interested in exploring everything and there are lots of ways you can help them discover things. They need your patience and understanding if things don't go smoothly, too. It's important to be sensitive to how babies feel if they fail when trying to do new things. Self-confidence is as vital for babies as it is for adults.

A blanket pegged over some chairs makes a simple play tent.

Indoor adventures

Setting up an obstacle course in a room for a baby provides a great adventure for them. It doesn't really matter how they get through it, or even if they don't, as long as they are enjoying exploring. There are some ideas for things to use on the left. Stay nearby, as some babies want help if they get stuck. Others prefer to work things out themselves. You could also try putting familiar small toys or baby books among the objects, to increase the interest for babies. They can decide for themselves whether to stop and play with them or not.

A mound of cushions can be plowed through, or scrambled over.

Let babies decide when to move, and when to take a break, as they explore.

An empty laundry basket turned on its side can make an exciting cave.

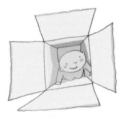

Large cardboard boxes are often popular with crawling babies.

Climbing stairs

A fascination with climbing, especially up stairs, can bring particular risks at this stage. Babies need to learn how to get up and down stairs safely, so set aside some time to show them how. A stair gate, across the bottom of stairs, prevents them from climbing when you can't watch them. When you do let them climb up a stair or two, stay behind them in case they lean over backward. You should have a stair gate at the top and bottom of stairs, so that you decide when babies go down. Spend time showing a baby how to come down, sliding backward on their tummies.

Stay close behind as a baby starts to climb stairs.

Babies will not be able to stand upright for long at first.

Getting upright

Before long, inquisitive, crawling babies want to see what is on that chair, or on that shelf. They start to pull themselves upright, which is both a huge effort, and a big thrill, for them – when they succeed of course.

The top half of a baby's body is much stronger than the bottom half, which means they can often pull themselves up, but their leg muscles are not strong enough to support them there for long. Let them use your legs, sturdy furniture or toys, crib bars and playpens to pull themselves up, and help them down again, if necessary.

Babies soon plop themselves down again if they feel tired.

For a cruising baby, any nearby object becomes something to grab onto.

Up and away

Although some babies don't take their first steps until they are well over a year old, others move straight from crawling to walking. Most spend some time shuffling around, holding on to things, before they really walk. This stage is known as cruising. Cruising babies need plenty of praise for their efforts, and help if they need it. They may have lots of tumbles, and need reassurance. The coordination skills they are learning are not easy to master.

Cruise time

Try putting chairs in a line with a slight gap between them. Let the baby cruise around them, then, after a while, move them a little farther apart to let the baby have a brief experience of standing. Some babies enjoy busily getting up, sitting down, and cruising around things. Try just relaxing on the sofa and letting them try these movements around you. Once a baby has taken a few steps on their own, some simple activities may help build their confidence and proficiency. Three ideas are listed on the left.

• Sit on the floor in front of the baby. Open your arms and call them over for a hug or a tickle.

• Hold both their hands and go for a walk. Now let them hold just your fingers, then only one hand.

• Wait until they are steady, then gently walk beside them. Be ready to catch them if they fall.

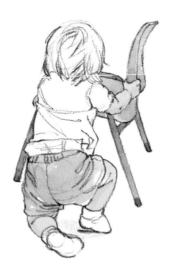

Cruising babies repeatedly heave themselves into an upright position.

With time, their need to hold on to something to stay upright will lessen.

Slowly does it

Caring for a newly walking baby has its pros and cons. You may have to carry the baby less, but may have to go everywhere very, very slowly. The baby may be happy to walk, but not necessarily where you need to go. If you can, give a new walker opportunities to go wherever they want to go, when you are not in a hurry. For them, walking is fun, so try to be understanding. If you can, allow babies to spend as much time as possible barefoot at this stage, so that the muscles of their toes and feet are fully exercised.

A tumble, a change in daily life or a minor illness can see a new walker going back to crawling for a while. They may feel more secure like that, but they will soon be up on their feet again.

Walking safely

You can buy socks with non-slip soles for newly walking babies. Ordinary socks on smooth floors are not safe, as the baby could slip. There are toys designed for them too, but some are more helpful than others.

- Pull-along toys are fun for babies who crawl well or can take a few steps. But make sure no one gets their legs tangled in string or cords.

- Some wheeled push-along toys can move too fast for a baby to keep up. Save them until the baby can walk confidently behind them.

- Sit-in baby-walkers with wheels are not recommended. They can be very dangerous, as they can tip over and injure a baby.

- Health experts also believe that sit-in walkers don't help babies learn to walk by themselves and might even hinder leg development.

Safety point
If you take a walking baby out, make sure you always hold their hand.

All about me

Babies are often fascinated with what people say and do, but they tend to be especially interested in themselves. This is a normal and important part of their development. On these pages are some activities inspired by babies' interest in themselves and some designed to help them find out more about other people, and learn to relate to them.

Babies may now watch the activities of other people with interest for several minutes.

They start to discover different parts of their bodies, such as their ears.

Who am I?

Most babies recognize their own name by around seven months and by about nine months, they may well have a 'name' they call people who they see a lot, although they may not be able to say it very clearly as yet.

You can help babies learn peoples' names by saying them often. Saying 'Ella needs a drink' or 'Here's Grandma!' helps a baby connect that word with that person. Looking at photos of family and friends is never boring for a baby, and also helps to reinforce who's who in their world. Point to the picture of each person, then say the person's name clearly.

By this stage, most babies are all too willing to let you know when they need, or want, something.

Useful tip

Babies may say words that are made-up, or not quite right. Don't correct them if this happens, just use the 'right' version when you say the word, so that they hear it.

Speaking up

Babies' first words are almost always their way of describing things that are important to them, such as a toy or a spoon. They have heard this word so many times that they feel able to try saying it. Many babies say several words during these months.

Give and take games

Babies at this stage often enjoy playing games involving giving and taking. They are too young to understand the concepts of sharing and taking turns, but can grasp that other people have things too. If you ask 'Can I have the ball?', a baby may pass it to you. If you return it with 'Now Sam can have it.', you can see if they pass it to you again. Games with food are fun too. Try 'One for Anna, and one for Daddy', as you pop a raisin into each of your mouths.

Which part is which?

Songs and rhymes that involve parts of the body are perfect for babies of this age. The song 'Head, shoulders, knees and toes' (see page 117) is often popular, as babies love to find the different parts of themselves.

Babies are very interested in their bodies. They may reach down to explore when you take off their diapers, suck their toes or pull their ears. This is all perfectly natural. To help a baby learn which part is which, try this activity:

1. Stand in front of a mirror. Point to your mouth and say 'Here's my mouth.'

2. Point to the baby's own mouth and say, clearly, 'Here's Sara's mouth.'

3. Now ask 'Where's Sara's mouth?' Gently move the baby's finger, if needed.

4. Repeat this with nose, eyes and ears, saying the 'body' words really clearly.

Balls are good for playing giving and taking games for babies in this age group.

Meeting other people

Babies' attitudes to meeting new people can differ hugely. Some are happy to see new faces. Others cling to people they know and are reluctant to greet anyone new. This is normal at this age. If you can, invite other people around, or go to baby and toddler groups. Even at this stage, babies can start to learn skills they need to play together.

Beginning around nine months old, babies may start to wave 'bye-bye' to people.

The great outdoors

Babies grab any chance to explore, and being outside gives them a whole new world to get to know. Research shows that children learn best if they are given the chance to try out new experiences regularly, so let babies spend some time outdoors as often as you can.

Visit your local park, take a trip to the store, or just take a walk together down the road. A baby will always find new things to entertain and interest them. Most babies love the sensation of gently swinging on baby swings in the playground or just having time to walk at their own pace.

Babies can go anywhere in a car seat, as long as it isn't too heavy for you to carry.

There are always lots of new and exciting things for a baby to see while safely strapped into the seat of a shopping cart.

• Splashing in warm water in a kiddie pool is most babies' idea of paradise and you can let them splash as vigorously as they want to outside.

• Give them plastic cups and a colander (or make holes in a yogurt container). They like to experiment by filling, emptying and drinking from them and watching the water trickling out of holes.

• Put some baby bubble bath in the water and hide objects that sink under the bubbles. Count each object as the baby finds it for you.

When you go out, try to set aside some time for babies to walk as fast, or as slowly, as they want to. They may want to close every gate along the street, or stop and pet a cat on the wall, but it's good to let them do so from time to time.

Fun with sand

Most babies will sit and play happily in sandbox for some time. They enjoy squeezing the sand, piling it into plastic cups and, if you are not careful, trying to eat it! Make sure it's always play sand or beach sand (not builders' sand).

Most babies will enjoy digging and scooping sand, and feeling its grainy texture.

• Ask babies to find small toys or shells half-buried in sand. They enjoy searching, and perfecting the picking-up 'pincer' movement with their fingers.

• Show babies how to make little sand castles with plastic cups. They will soon discover that knocking them down is satisfying, as well!

Safety point

Never leave babies unattended in sandboxes or kiddie pools and always protect them from the sun with sunscreen.

Ball games

Balls are very versatile toys to play with in a pool or in a big space, such as a park. Learning all the skills that are involved in picking up and holding a ball, or rolling it to someone else, can take some practice. Try some of these first, easy baby ball games using a big, soft ball:

Sit opposite the baby and roll the ball over to them. Ask them to roll it back to you. Move a little farther away each time you both successfully get the ball.

Show the baby how to lie on top of a big ball and roll gently backward and forward. They may roll right off it, but they won't fall far.

Kicking involves taking one foot off the ground, which is tricky. If you kick a ball to the baby, encourage them to shuffle it back with both feet.

Going swimming

For most babies of this age, there are few activities that are more enjoyable than going swimming. Of course, they will not swim properly for a long time, but the sooner you take them to your local pool the better, as it will become a familiar place, and one they'll like visiting. Basic confidence in the water will really help them when they learn to swim in the future.

Remember to take spare diapers and wipes as well as swim diapers to the pool.

• Find out if the pool has a baby and toddler pool. It will be warmer, and just for babies and caregivers.

• Experts don't advise using blow-up seats or anything else to help babies stay afloat in water at this stage. That's your job, all the time.

• Take two swim diapers, and take a towel to the side of the pool. Babies lose heat fast, and need wrapping up as soon as they're out.

• If you have to go down a ladder into the pool, hand the baby to another adult until you are in the water, in case you slip.

• Some babies feel more secure if you take some bath toys from home (but be sure they float...)

• A few babies are unsure at first, or dislike being splashed in the face. They usually overcome these feelings after a while.

It's good for babies to get used to being in the water without any flotation aid, but take care and hold on to them at all times.

Be prepared

Although you should not be in the water for longer than about 20 minutes, taking babies swimming does need a little advance planning. If the baby is tired or unwell, leave it until another day. On the left are some tips on things to do and take to make sure your trip to the pool is enjoyable.

Swim lessons

Many pools offer baby and toddler swim classes, led by a trained instructor. These are intended to guide you as you introduce a baby to pre-swimming skills. Full of songs and games, they may help babies who are not so sure about the water.

Water games

Playing in the water uses lots of muscles in the body, and is excellent all-round exercise. Take it slowly, and make sure you stay low down in the water next to the baby, so that they feel happy and safe. It's vital to make these experiences positive ones for them. Here are some games to try:

Water games are fun as well as good exercise for babies.

Staying low in the water, hold the baby securely under their arms and twirl them gently around.

Rest the top of their body on your chest, hold their legs and move them up and down, saying, 'Kick, kick!' to encourage kicking.

Let them lean their head on your shoulder and their face against yours. Stretch your arms under their legs as they float.

Holding the baby under the arms, whoosh them up out of the water and then down again. This helps them get used to splashes.

Getting dressed

Don't leave a baby of this age on a changing table while you get dressed, in case they roll off. Put them in a playpen or strap-in baby seat, if there is one. If there isn't, sit them on the floor once they're dressed.

Don't forget to take a drink and snack to the pool for after the swim.

Baby's first birthday

Children are unlikely to remember anything about their first year when they're older, but it will have been an amazing 12 months for everyone caring for them. You may want to celebrate their birthday in style, but try to remember that, for a one-year old, a balloon and crinkly giftwrap are enough to make the day exciting. If you want to throw a party, inviting a few baby friends (each with an adult), could work well. On the left are some tips for a first party.

Keep food simple and try not to do too much; this is not the time to try new tastes. Make sure there are enough adults to supervise the babies eating, and clear leftovers away promptly. Avoid things with lots of sugar. A few treats are fine, but too many may affect babies' moods. Here are a few suggestions for foods to serve for babies who are ready:

- *Make sure the party venue is child-proofed for safety as most of the guests will be crawling.*

- *Choose your time well, avoiding guests' nap times if you can. Try to serve food at a mealtime.*

- *Keep the party no longer than 1 to 1¹/₂ hours. This is long enough for one-year olds.*

- *Find out if any guest is allergic to certain foods, and don't be hurt if some seem fussy eaters.*

- *Supervise guests playing freely. They may enjoy playing with giftwrap or the birthday baby's toys.*

- *Include time to sing songs and rhymes. This is a calming activity, after food, for instance.*

- *chopped or mashed banana*
- *seedless grapes (quartered)*
- *pizza (in small squares)*
- *cupcakes*

- *ice cream*
- *small cubes of cheese*
- *little sandwiches*

An older child may like to help the baby blow out their candle.

Toddler time

During the six months following their first birthday, most children leave the baby stage and become a 'toddler' (which describes their toddling, early steps). A key thing to remember is that most toddlers make it very clear if they are not interested in doing something, so don't get stressed trying to get them to do an activity – leave it until another day.

How will my baby change?

Toddlers are able to say more words, and understand even more. They will understand simple instructions, too.

Some children begin feeding and undressing themselves. Some will let you know when they need to go to the bathroom... or have just been.

Toddlers begin to learn social skills, such as playing with other children. Sharing can be tricky to learn, though.

A toddler may show an interest in creating things, such as pretend food from play dough or marks on paper with crayons.

There may be bursts of real anger if things do not go as a toddler wants them to.

Books get sucked, chewed, and bitten. Check them often, wipe them clean and throw out any too germy to save.

Useful tip

As a toddler learns the fun that can be had from books, try leaving some favorites in their crib. They may enjoy looking at them after a nap, or before falling asleep.

• Friends with children may suggest books that their children enjoy.

• Libraries keep a good selection for this age group and most bookstores have titles that they recommend.

• You could visit the Usborne Quicklinks Website at www.usborne-quicklinks.com Type in the keywords 'babies and books' for more ideas.

More about books

For a toddler, there are few toys that can give as much pleasure as a well-chosen book. Research shows that sharing books with toddlers between 12 and 18 months can help them begin to develop the literacy skills they will need throughout life. The main thing to remember as you look at books with toddlers is that your goal is to help give them a lasting enjoyment of books and what's inside them.

Why look at books?

Put simply, books give children the chance to learn about how pages turn and to follow simple stories. They allow them to hear new words and to practice the ones they know. They help them learn how to listen when someone reads and how to recognize the people, animals and objects in pictures.

Toddlers often prefer to look at pictures of things that they know about, such as vehicles and toys.

Know a good book?

With so many books available, it can be hard to guess which ones toddlers will enjoy. Simple stories, nursery rhymes, and books with puzzles, flaps, sounds or pop-ups are often popular, or you could try some factual books about farms and animals or diggers and trucks.

Learning to love books

It's easier to get the most out of looking at books with a toddler if you bear a few guidelines in mind. Pick your time for sharing a book. A quiet half hour after a meal, before a nap, or at bedtime is ideal as a restless toddler won't enjoy having to sit still. As you look at the book, point things out and encourage the child to do so too. Most toddlers will recognize and point to more and more things they see in their books.

• Try leaving out the last word of a story or nursery rhyme, and waiting for the child to add it. This early predictive skill helps with reading.

• Counting together helps children learn numbers. Encourage the toddler to point at things on the pages as you count them together.

• Let the toddler tell you about the pictures or story. Their interruptions show they are interested in the book, and thinking about it.

• Story CDs don't give a toddler the chance to snuggle up and share a book with you, but can be calming (and give you time to get a meal ready...).

As you share a book with a toddler, point out things on the page and talk about them.

Make a book box

Try putting some wipeable board books into a special box and keeping it in the room that a toddler plays in. This makes 'looking at books' an everyday activity, and one that children can enjoy by themselves. Make sure the box is sturdy but not so big that the toddler can't reach the books easily.

To make a toddler's book box more special, you could cover it in paper and label it.

What goes where?

Finding things to entertain and interest a child under 18 months old can be hard, especially if you're busy, and it can be tempting to buy expensive 'educational' toys that promise to answer both your needs. These pages try to help you choose toys that toddlers will enjoy playing with. That's the best way for them to learn, after all.

What are toys for?

Research has shown that children will play and make up games even if their only toys are twigs, pebbles or nothing at all. In some parts of the world, toddlers are already involved in stirring pots or flattening dough. These are all activities that they enjoy doing, with or without sophisticated toys. Some experts argue that toys don't teach children skills, but they can help them to practice them, so the best kinds of toys to offer a toddler are ones that let them do things, or try things out; interactive toys, in other words.

Toddlers are fascinated with things that can go into other things. An old shoe box as a bed for dolls or teddies is popular, for instance. Three more, simple, toys that will help toddlers find out that some things fit and others don't are listed above left.

- A toy train or bus with little people to slot inside is usually a big hit at this stage. Toddlers like pushing wheeled toys along, too.

- A shape sorter gives toddlers shapes to slot into holes and something to shake. Some may need help with what fits where.

- Plastic nesting cups can be fit inside each other or stacked into towers. They can also be used in the sandbox or bath.

Simple blocks that fit together can entertain a child for ages and help their coordination.

Shoe boxes make perfect beds for bunnies, dollies and teddy bears.

Toy corner

Toddlers often have strong ideas about what they want to play with. If you have room, keep a toy box with a small selection of toys in the room the toddler spends most time in. Let them choose which ones to get out, even if it means you have to put them all away later on.

Toddlers gain a lot by playing with an older child, or an adult.

Toddlers enjoy playing with toys that do something...

...or that they can do something with...

Include things such as a plastic spoon, a clean hairbrush and a plastic beaker in the box. Children at this stage are learning what everyday things are by seeing, and copying, what people do with them. Experts call this 'definition by use'. It's a good idea to change the toys in the toy box regularly, putting some away for a while.

Play with me!

Research shows that, if you or another adult or child plays with a toddler each day, even if it's only for a short time, they will gain a great deal from that experience. On the right are some suggestions for a few simple games you could try playing with them.

- Toddlers love to give you things and take them back. Add a cheery 'thank you' to this little game.

- Try hiding a toy and then revealing it with a 'Here it is!' Let the toddler have turns at this too.

- Action rhymes like 'Pat-a-cake' are ideal at this stage, as they're always the same, which toddlers love.

Once a toddler can fit things together...

...they may enjoy doing puzzles. Ones with pictures of familiar things are best first. Give them a hand if they need it.

Useful tip

If a child seems reluctant to play alone at this stage, don't force it. This is a big leap for them to make and trying to hurry them may have the opposite effect.

Playing alone

Between a year and 18 months old, most children start to play a little on their own – with a watchful adult nearby, of course. Encourage their first signs of independence by giving a toddler lots of opportunities to play on their own, but make sure they still have plenty of playtime with you.

First puzzles

Most toddlers enjoy first puzzles, or inset boards. These are chunky wooden shapes with pictures on them, which fit into cut-out spaces in a tray. Many have plastic knobs, to help the toddler pick them up. These puzzles are ideal, as, after a while, toddlers want to do them on their own.

Mastering all the skills needed to pick up a piece, then slot it into place takes time. You may need to show a child what to do a few times, but encourage their efforts and be patient with them.

Beads threaded on a thick wire may keep a toddler busy for quite a while.

Toys that involve threading beads or blocks along a wire are another kind of puzzle that often absorbs toddlers. These help them to develop hand-eye coordination, without any risk of them swallowing the small objects.

Building blocks

Some experts believe that children learn by playing with things again and again, coming back and playing with them in different ways as they develop. Building blocks are one of the toys that will provide play and enjoyment for a toddler for a long time – though you will notice that what a child does with their blocks will change considerably over time.

Do it yourself

Playing alone encourages children to use their imagination, and to try out things that interest them, in their own time. Providing a variety of 'new' things for them to play with helps this process. Below are a couple of suggestions to try. Playthings like these cost nothing, but will give most toddlers plenty to try out and practice.

• Let a toddler play with some empty food boxes, tubes and clean plastic pots instead of, or as well as, their toy building blocks.

• Try cutting holes big enough for small toys to fit through in the side of a large box and letting the toddler 'mail' their toys.

Until a child is about a year old, they may just put blocks in and out of a box, or bang them together.

By 18 months old, you may notice them building blocks into a tower before knocking it down.

Show toddlers how to build tracks for toy cars, pens for toy animals... or how to knock down towers.

It takes a great deal of concentration for a toddler to master building a tower.

Messy fun

Making a mess is most toddlers' idea of heaven, and they are blissfully unaware of how much work it can make for you. Experts have found that some young children pick up on adults' dislike of mess, and can develop anxieties about trying new things, so it's a good idea to try not to worry too much about keeping things neat and tidy.

Be prepared

Getting ready for a messy play session is essential, and will reduce your stress levels later on. On the left are three simple steps to follow before you begin.

Some toddlers so dislike getting their clothes dirty that they find it hard to enjoy messy play, or playing outdoors where there might be mud or water. Endless washing is tiresome for you, too, so either try to protect clothes before you begin, or – if it's warm at home – let them enjoy getting messy wearing just their diapers, and then have fun getting clean in the bathtub.

1. Spread a plastic sheet or newspaper under the toddler's chair and table, and over the table too.

2. Make sure both of you are wearing aprons, old clothes... or clothes that are easily washed.

3. Have a bowl of water and a cloth on hand just in case the paint hits the wall...

Safety point

Make sure you only let toddlers play with non-toxic, washable paint.

Plastic coveralls with elastic cuffs are ideal for messy play.

Messy food

Most babies thoroughly enjoy playing with food, so this activity is likely to be popular. They will relish the chance to feel the different textures and shapes. It can help overcome food fussiness, too. The list below shows some foods that you could try, but the choice is up to you. Try for a variety of tastes above all. Put a little of each food into small bowls and let the toddler have free rein to pick up, feel and try each one.

Exploring food may help toddlers overcome fussiness.

- cold, cooked pasta or rice
- crushed ice cubes
- orange segments
- cucumber chunks
- tiny cubes of gelatin
- bread crusts
- quartered olives
- carrot sticks
- very small cubes of cheese

Painting and splashing

Children between one year and 18 months old are too young to hold a paintbrush or to paint recognizable objects, but most of them will love the chance of playing with some paint, so finger painting is ideal at this stage. On the right are some more messy activities to try, either outdoors or inside – but make sure you cover the floor well with newspaper or a plastic sheet.

- Let them spend time filling and emptying cups and containers in a large plastic bowl of water.

- Try adding a few drops of food coloring to the water, so they can see it flowing easily from cup to cup.

- Mix up cornflour and water in a tray. Toddlers love splashing hands in it and squishing it.

While older children can use a brush and hands for painting, younger ones can paint with fingers.

Safety point

Always stay close by when toddlers are playing with water.

Home help

Home should be a safe, familiar place for a toddler, where they can watch all the comings and goings with interest. As they near 18 months old, many children develop a fascination with household jobs, such as cooking and cleaning. You may find they want to do these jobs with you, or for you. On these pages are some ways of encouraging their curiosity.

Give a toddler a duster and let them dust a low surface (without any breakables on it…).

Toddlers won't sweep the floor perfectly, but it's important to give their efforts lots of praise.

• Let your toddler put some fruit into a bowl, shoes onto a rack or clothes in the dryer.

• When emptying the dryer, leave a few small items in it; and let them put the items in the laundry basket.

• If they want to help you wash the car, put a plastic apron on them, give them a sponge and prepare for them to get wet.

Can I do it?

It seems unlikely that toddlers are interested in chores because they want to keep things neat and clean. What fascinates them are the actions involved: pushing and pulling, sweeping and dusting, emptying and filling. Experts agree that children learn a huge amount by copying what they see, so give them the chance to try things themselves. They will take ages to do each chore (and you will have to do it yourself later), but try to praise their efforts to help.

Toy tools

There are many toy versions of household equipment available. They let a toddler safely work alongside you. Smaller toys, such as a set of plastic pans, a dustpan and brush and a toy telephone, are not expensive, and will provide a lot of enjoyment for a busy toddler. Larger toy equipment, such as mini kitchens, can be more costly, but you may find one at a garage sale or consignment store. Many toddlers will play just as happily with an oven made from a box.

Try using an old box and some tape and pens to make a simple toy oven.

Home from home

Most toddlers love playing in their own den or playhouse, and it's good to give them the chance to play in a safe, secret place. You don't need to buy an expensive playhouse – some blankets fastened with clothespins to two sturdy chairs will be fine. They may just go in and out repeatedly at first; let them explore in their own way. Many toddlers progress to playing simple make-believe games in their playhouses, such as feeding toys with spoons. Research shows that children understand things in everyday life through make-believe play like this.

Any den is exciting for toddlers because it's different, private – and theirs.

• If a toddler is tired, either 'build' a nap in the stroller or car into your plans, or wait until they have had a nap before leaving.

• Take drinks and food with you if you will be out for some time. This allows you to avoid having to buy snacks in a store or café.

• Don't plan too long an activity. Toddlers love variety, but get tired of taking in new sights and sounds more quickly than you do.

• Keep it simple: the main goal is for you both to get out, get some fresh air and exercise and enjoy each other's company.

Useful tip
Toddlers tend to whine if they are bored. Adding a variety of interesting and engaging activities to your daily routine is helpful.

Let's go out

Finding enough things to do to entertain a curious, energetic toddler can be a tall order. A change of scene can help prevent a bored child from becoming a bad-tempered one. These pages try to give you some ideas for going out with a toddler that will keep them happy without costing you a fortune. Just as when they were tiny, you need to plan an outing carefully, but it's worth it.

Getting ready to go

It is not always easy to predict a toddler's mood and ensure a successful trip, but there are a few things it's helpful to bear in mind before you set out. There are some suggestions for ways of reducing stress on the left.

Toddlers find the simplest of new experiences totally absorbing.

Where shall we go?

A trip to a pet store is exciting for a toddler and most pet store owners are happy for them to visit their animals as long as they don't bang the glass tanks or cages. Taking a toddler swimming gives them exercise, a change of scene and a stimulating experience. On the right are some other suggestions for places to go.

Staying calm

Although childcare professionals usually reserve the word 'tantrum' for older toddlers, of around two years old, an 18-month old can do a good job of spoiling your outing together, too. Trying to strap a howling child into a stroller in public can make you less willing to venture out again. Below are some tactics to try out if a child is not behaving as you'd wish.

• If you're lucky enough to live near some woods or a beach, toddlers may love exploring, and finding treasures such as leaves or shells.

• Shopping has to be done, but is not very exciting for toddlers. Stop at a park or playground after errands, so they know the fun comes after the boring part.

• A ride on a bus gives toddlers plenty of new experiences. Insist they sit properly (or they'll go in their stroller) and talk about all the things you see.

• A picnic in a nearby outdoor space is far more exciting than another meal at home. If the weather's fine, pack some food, a blanket and ball and head off.

• Stay calm and keep your voice low and steady.

• Distract their attention by pointing out something else.

• Take deep breaths and know that their outburst will end.

• Gently take the toddler away from the situation.

• If you are feeling brave, just ignore the tantrum entirely.

• Remember that you're the boss and you set the rules.

Talk about it

Talk to a toddler about all the things that you did together at the end of the day, even if it hasn't been particularly unusual. Quite simply, this shows that their experiences and feelings matter to you, and they will understand more of what you say to them than you realize.

Toddlers will be tired after a busy day because they are learning so much, so fast.

Keep moving

The only time most toddlers stop moving, or wanting to move, is when they are asleep or sick. This incredible amount of energy can cause problems if you have limited space at home for them to run around in. Here are some ideas to help them get some active play.

Walk and talk... and soft play

Walking is good exercise, and still a novelty, for most toddlers. As their confidence grows, encourage them to walk alongside you whenever you can. Insist they hold on to the stroller, or your hand, though. The more chances you give toddlers to walk, the more they'll want to. Remember that they can't learn to walk faster, or better, in a stroller. Point out things you see as you walk along.

'I'm coming to get you' tag games usually see toddlers run squealing away. It's best played outside, unless your home is obstacle-free.

Draw some circles of different sizes in chalk on the ground outside. Hold a toddler's hand and jump from one circle to another.

Useful tip

Find out if there's a baby gym class nearby. They're not expensive and most toddlers enjoy them.

Toddlers have as much curiosity as they have energy. Keep an eye on them as they explore.

Many toddlers enjoy soft play centers. These are specially designed to entertain the most active of toddlers in safety. If you have space, you could set up a simple version at home, with cushions, air beds or mattresses.

Active toys

Toys that promote active play come in many shapes and sizes. Toddlers don't need an aerobic workout to get some healthy, energy-using play or improve their coordination skills. There are some ideas on the right.

Toys that toddlers can push or pull will keep them moving.

• Different-sized balls are great for rolling, trying to kick, or just picking up and running with. Beach balls can be fun for them to catch, too.

• By 18 months, many toddlers enjoy toys they can ride on and push along with their feet. Choose a safe model, and always supervise as they ride.

• Visit a local playground to use play equipment, such as swings, slides, seesaws and jungle gyms (but be sure to keep a close eye on them).

Toddler gymnastics

Toddlers' bodies are extremely flexible and you may find that they can bend and stretch far more easily than you can. Below are some ideas for simple gymnastics you could try with them. Always be gentle, and stop if a child is unsure or if you feel uncomfortable.

Lie down with your knees bent. Get the toddler to lean on your legs, and hold their hands. Gently lift your legs.

To go higher, you could hold the toddler's shoulders to stop them from sliding forward into your face.

Sit with the toddler between your knees. Keeping one of their legs bent, help them lift the other leg.

Let them kiss their toes, then try the other foot. Now let them lean back against you and kiss both their own feet.

• Only let toddlers watch programs specifically designed to appeal to their age group. These usually contain a mixture of familiar words and ideas, and some new ones.

• Don't let them watch for long. Their concentration span is limited, and they'll absorb and enjoy less if they are 'parked' in front of the TV for longer than about 15 minutes.

Toddlers and TV

There is a lot of debate among experts about whether it's a good idea to let toddlers watch TV. Research shows that watching too much TV, or unsuitable programs, can hinder children's development in several ways. Overall, until a child is two years old, it's important to limit their watching time pretty strictly. If you decide to let a toddler watch TV, it's worth bearing a few points in mind. Whatever you decide, remember that a toddler will never gain as much from watching TV as they will from playing.

DVDs and videos

Some experts believe that it's better for young children to watch suitable DVDs or videos rather than TV programs. Toddlers respond well to constant repetition, so they don't mind watching the same thing many times. The content of the DVD is then known by the child, and – importantly – by you. DVDs that contain simple stories, sing-along songs or rhymes are especially suitable. Ones featuring specific characters can be limiting, but toddlers enjoy them. As with TV, make sure you keep an eye on how long they watch.

If you can, watch a TV program with your child. Talk to them about what you see and explain any new things.

Useful tip

It's not a good idea to have a TV in a young child's bedroom. They could watch unsuitable programs once they can turn it on, and their bedroom is for sleeping in.

A wider world

Between 18 months and two years old,
a toddler's vocabulary will grow very rapidly.
You may hear them trying to say new words
almost every day and they will understand much
more of what you say to them, too. During these
months, many toddlers make great strides
toward becoming an individual, with likes
and dislikes all of their own.

How will my toddler change?

Toddlers begin to put two words together during
these months, to make short sentences.

Most toddlers will play alongside other children, but rarely
with them. They are still learning social skills.

Toys that have knobs, handles and parts that fit together
are fascinating. They may absorb a child for ages.

By two years old, toddlers love scrambling up
playground equipment, stairs... and furniture.

At this stage, toddlers begin to master feeding
themselves and using a cup properly.

They may almost be able to dress themselves.

Shapes and sizes

During this stage, most toddlers are interested in putting things into some sort of size order, and try out what fits inside what. This process is called classifying. As toddlers' hand-eye coordination improves, they enjoy making things of different shapes and sizes, be it from boxes, bottles, sand or dough. The activities on these pages focus on their interest in the shape, and size, of things around them. The more you use words such as 'big', 'small', 'circle' and 'square' for things you see in everyday life, the quicker toddlers will understand the idea of shape and size. On the left are some ways of helping toddlers learn these concepts through play.

• Keep a collection of different-sized boxes, tubes and plastic pots and trays. Help the toddler put them in size order, saying the shape and size of each thing.

• Try helping them tape some boxes, cardboard tubes or yogurt containers together. Talk about what shape each object is and what you could be making.

• Cut some simple shapes out of thin cardboard. Let toddlers lay the shapes out on a flat surface, name each one, and see what pictures you can both make.

• If you have a sandbox, or can visit a beach, most toddlers will spend ages pressing sand into molds, plastic cups and buckets of different sizes.

A set of building blocks is an ideal toy for toddlers finding out about shapes.

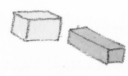

Look in a book

Many toddlers' books have pictures of things in different shapes and sizes, which make things clearer for children as they try to put the things they see in order in their minds. Move the toddler's finger around the shapes as you name them, saying 'This is a circle,' or 'Here's a square.' Try looking at a book and asking a toddler 'Where's a big dog?' or 'Can you find the little car for me?'

Pictures of shapes in books may not interest you, but they do appeal to toddlers and help them to learn about shapes and sizes.

Play dough

Play dough is one of the toys that young children play with in different ways at different stages of their development. It has what experts call a long 'play life' and is suitable for children starting at about 18 months. Toddlers younger than two years old will probably not be able to make recognizable models, but they will enjoy squeezing and shaping the dough.

It's easy to make your own play dough. Kept in a plastic bag or sealed container in the refrigerator, it will last for several months. There is a recipe for homemade play dough on the Usborne Quicklinks Website (see page 118).

Things to do with dough

A play dough session gives a toddler the chance to squeeze, flatten, tear, roll and press. This is not only great fun; it also gives them the chance to see the effect of their actions on something else, which is valuable. On the right are some ideas to try after the toddler has enjoyed playing with the dough 'their way' for a while. Always play with play dough at a table, or on a large tray. Cover the floor underneath and put an apron on the toddler. Tie back long hair, too, as dough can get stuck in it, harden... and need cutting out later.

Safety point

Toddlers may try to eat play dough, so make sure you always supervise while they're playing with it.

• Make some really simple models, such as a ball, an apple or a banana, and see if the toddler can recognize what they are.

• Roll some dough out flat and let them press patterns into it with cookie cutters, a plastic fork, or with their fingers.

• Toddlers know body parts, so try making a simple model of a person and naming its nose, eyes, mouth, arms and legs.

Most toddlers love playing with dough and happily squash and pummel it for ages.

Time to get dressed

Toddlers under the age of two years old can't usually dress and undress themselves – but this doesn't stop them from trying. This fascination with taking clothes on and off can be a little irritating, but don't forget that they do need to practice if they are ever going to do the job themselves.

'Me do it!'

Many adults caring for toddlers have been driven to despair by the three little words: 'Me do it'. They know that they usually come before a huge clash of wills, as the determined toddler tries to get dressed and won't be helped. On the left are some tips for heading off these problems.

Toddlers enjoy trying on all kinds of clothes. Keep a box of old hats, handbags, scarves and chunky jewelry for them to play with. Consignment stores are good places to buy these things cheaply.

• Make times for toddlers to dress and undress when you're not in a hurry. Show them how zippers and buttons work.

• Agree on a compromise. Let the toddler pull their T-shirt on but say clearly that you are going to button their pants up.

• Shoes can be especially problematic. Try distracting a toddler as you quickly slip them on, or say you'll 'do' one foot each.

• Have a regular dressing play session. Give toddlers a selection of clothes, and let them play with them – socks on hands are fine.

A box of old accessories offers a toddler plenty of play opportunities.

Toddlers need a lot of practice to master all the skills they need to get dressed by themselves.

Toy love

Toddlers often want to bathe and feed their toys, chat with them and respond to their imagined needs. They may copy the way they have seen you behave. Many experts feel that it's important for children to form these emotional bonds with some toys. The comfort they feel when they play with them is invaluable.

Many toddlers – both boys and girls – enjoy dressing and undressing dolls, or soft toys. This is easier for them if the clothes are easy to do up and undo. Some toys are designed to give toddlers practice in the fastenings found on real clothes. These can be useful, but take them away if children find them too hard and get frustrated.

Useful tip
Remember that toy clothes get dirty too and need to be washed in warm, soapy water from time to time.

Many toddlers have firm views about just how they want their dolls' hair, or clothes, to look.

Toddlers respond as if to a real person if you 'do the voice' of a toy.

Choosing clothes

For some toddlers, what they wear is of great importance. They may refuse to let themselves be dressed in certain clothes, choosing ones that may not be suitable for the weather, or for the activities of the day ahead. This can be maddening, but try to remember to praise them when they get something right, such as putting on a hat when it's cold. On the right are some other tactics to try when you find yourself having to deal with this tricky behavior.

• Decide if a battle over clothes is worth fighting. If the clothes are warm or cool enough, does it really matter if they don't match?

• If you really can't agree to their choice, stay calm as you put them into other clothes, firmly saying, 'No – you need to wear these today'.

• Try just limiting the number of choices. Offer a maximum of three outfits, let the toddler choose one and put the others away quickly.

• Pieces of sponge, cardboard, scrunched-up tissue paper, pieces of cloth or just hands are all ideal for getting paint onto paper.

• The spongy part of a decorator's paint roller or medium-sized paintbrush may be easier for little hands to grip.

• As toddlers' coordination improves, encourage them to make fingerprints rather than whole handprints. Try some fingerprint patterns.

• Mix paint with lots of water and let toddlers wash it onto paper with a sponge. They could do this over wax-crayon pictures, too.

Useful tip
At this stage, toddlers may get paint on their faces and in their hair. Doing painting near bathtime might be a good idea.

Toddler painting

Most toddlers want to show what they think and feel in as many different ways as they can. Art activities give them a chance to express their view of the world through the pictures they produce. Here are some ideas for painting with toddlers up to two years old. You don't need to be artistic yourself, or buy lots of equipment. The focus is on having fun with paint.

Making marks

Most toddlers love painting because they can make something visually satisfying very quickly. If they still find holding a paintbrush tricky, there are four other ways to help them make their mark with paint on the left.

Toy stores sell tough, plastic aprons that are ideal for toddler painting sessions.

Cut-up bath sponges are good for dipping into paint and making marks.

When toddlers paint, they will get messy, but their enjoyment makes the inevitable clean up afterward worth it. Buy washable, non-toxic paints, and follow the steps on page 56 before you start, to make things easier.

What is it?

One of the reasons why art activities are so valuable is that they give toddlers a chance to show you the way they see things. Their picture of a car may not look like one to you, but to them, at this stage, it does. When they tell you what their picture shows, it doesn't matter that it's not realistic and it's important to encourage their creativity by praising their efforts. They'll have learned a lot by trying to get what they see onto paper.

• Congratulate them, and show interest in what they are doing and in the finished thing they bring to show you.

• Talk to toddlers about the things they have made. Tell them which parts and colors you like best, and why.

• Don't throw pictures away. To the child, they are special; try to display them at home (for a few days, at least).

Art activities help toddlers to think about the world around them.

When toddlers start painting with brushes, supply a chunky brush for each color.

Water painting

You don't even need paint for a toddler to enjoy painting. Water can be just as good at letting them create something that they find satisfying. Below are three water-painting ideas. It's best to do them outside on a warm, dry day.

Stick some paper to a fence or wall. Give the toddler a bucket of water and a big brush, roller or sponge to make pictures.

If you have access to a porch or sidewalk, toddlers like making water pictures on them and watching them vanish as they dry.

Dribbling water out of a watering can is fun, too. Help toddlers form a circle, square or whatever shape they choose.

All about colors

For toddlers, the world is an exciting, colorful place. Between 18 months and two years old, most toddlers begin to show interest in, and learn, the names of the colors they see around them. Games with colors often prove really popular with children at this stage. Here are some simple ways of reinforcing the names of basic colors as you go about your daily life together:

1. Before you go out on a color walk, show the toddler something that is the color you'll be hunting for.

• Call things by color as toddlers play with them, by saying 'Here's a purple block.' or 'This one's red.'

• Play color games, asking a toddler to 'Find me a yellow ring,' or 'Put all the green blocks in here.'

• Try letting a toddler choose what color T-shirt or socks to wear, (but limit them to three possibilities).

2. As you walk, point out things of the color you've chosen, saying 'There's a blue door,' or 'Here's a blue flower.'

3. Ask the toddler to spot something blue for you. Try playing 'I spy a car that is blue – can you?' as a clue.

Ask a toddler if they can choose a red toy to go with the red car.

Color walks

4. On your way back, you could ask them if they remember where the 'blue door' (for example) was.

Another entertaining way of helping toddlers to learn colors is to take them out on a 'color walk'. Most toddlers will enjoy the experience and hunt for colored things avidly. You'll find some helpful hints down the left-hand side of this page. If it works well, try setting out again to look for things in another color.

Food fun

There are plenty of foods that are naturally colorful, such as red cherry tomatoes and orange carrots. Playing food color games may encourage toddlers to try something new (but avoid using artificially colored foods if you can).

You could try putting food of different colors onto separate plates and covering each one with a paper towel. Take the paper off one plate at a time, and talk about what color all the food is before you let them eat it. Finding blue food might be tricky, but there are some other ideas to try on the right.

Toys and books

Most toys for toddlers, such as blocks, stacking rings and pop-together beads, are very brightly colored, which they seem to find attractive. Many books for this stage of development focus on colors, too. Spend time together spotting 'six red things' or 'a yellow duck' on a page.

Colorful blocks make it easy for you to name the colors again and again for a toddler.

Orange foods:
• Orange segments
• Small cubes of orange cheese
• Cooked sweet potato (cubed)
• Pieces of orange pepper
• Carrots sticks

Green foods:
• Cucumber (cubed)
• Green apple (sliced)
• Green grapes (quartered)
• Avocado (sliced)
• Green pepper (sliced)

Red foods:
• Red apple (sliced)
• Cherry tomatoes (quartered)
• Red grapes (quartered)
• Pieces of red pepper
• Strawberries (quartered)

1. Sit on a blanket or bench and, keeping the toddler in view, ask them to bring you a flower, a leaf, or a stick.

2. Show an interest in their finds. Talk about each one and maybe take them home. For toddlers, they are treasures.

3. Try to make sure they don't pick up anything dirty. Just in case, wash their hands afterward.

Small companions

As toddlers approach two, many start to become little companions, happy to play alongside you more. They will probably chat away with you, too, though you may not understand all they say yet. These activities try to entertain and interest a toddler at home, or when you are both out and about.

Can you find it?

By this stage most toddlers understand far more words than they can say. If you ask them to find something for you, such as their shoes, they may well do so, even if they have never said the word 'shoes'. In a store you could ask them to spot bananas or apples on the shelves for you. Most toddlers will really enjoy feeling they are helping you in some way. If you have a yard or garden, or can visit an outdoor space, you could continue the activity with a nature hunt. There are some suggestions for what to do on the left.

Searching for nuts in fall is a real treasure hunt for toddlers.

Wildlife watch

Many toddlers are fascinated with animals, birds and, especially, bugs. At this age, it is probably best to discourage children from picking up small creatures as their fingers may squash them simply because they cannot control how hard they grip small objects. They may still try to eat them, too.

Look for spiders' webs. Small children are often fascinated by them.

• Encourage them to watch animals as they crawl, wiggle or fly.

• Count spiders' legs and talk about their round bodies or hairy legs.

• Give ants crumbs to carry and watch where they take them.

• A magnifying glass makes looking at bugs even better.

Helping out

Toddlers under two cannot really cook with you yet, but if you give them an absorbing activity to do in the kitchen alongside you, they will feel involved. Try these ideas to make them feel like they are 'cooking'.

Safety point

Never leave toddlers unsupervised in the kitchen, even if they are absorbed in what they are doing. Accidents happen quickly.

• Give them a plastic bowl, a wooden spoon and some uncooked pasta to stir.

• Let them sort the fruit out, putting apples, bananas and oranges into different bowls.

• They could thread dried fruit rings, or hooped cereal, onto string, for you to knot.

• Provide some real food, water, plastic plates and cups and let them hold a tea party.

Useful tip

Getting everything ready before you start is part of the fun for toddlers, so let them help you set up.

1. Put some everyday objects, such as dried pasta, cotton balls, string or fabric, foil and leaves on some plastic plates.

2. Brush craft glue over a big piece of cardboard or thick paper. Add more if it dries before the picture is finished.

3. Encourage the toddler to glue things on. Show them how to curl string, or glue things on top of each other.

Everyday art

Research shows that toddlers benefit from having some sort of routine to their day, and it's a good idea for them to do different kinds of play activities at different times of the day. The activities on these pages are for quieter times, as they involve sitting down and concentrating. The things toddlers make may not seem like art to you – but each one gives you a little insight into how they feel, learn and think.

Toddlers will enjoy choosing the size, shape and color of what they want to use in their pictures.

Stick to it

Most toddlers of between 18 months and two years enjoy gluing things onto paper. At this stage, toddlers find using scissors too hard, so you need to cut things out for them, but let them do the gluing. For the ideas below, it can be less messy if toddlers use a solid glue stick.

• Cut faces out of a magazine or comic. Let the toddler put glue on the back, and glue them down on a sheet of paper.

• Toddlers like tearing paper into pieces or strips, ready to glue down. Give them old magazines, or tissue paper to tear.

• Paper or cardboard food packaging cut into pieces can be used to make a collage picture you can talk about.

To glue down things that are heavier than paper, such as those suggested on the left, you'll need non-toxic white glue, which dries clear. Toddlers of this age may find it hard to control a glue brush, so it's best if you take charge of smearing the glue onto the sheet of paper or cardboard.

Plates and packaging

A package of cheap, plain paper plates, some cotton balls or yarn, tissue paper and a selection of food packaging can provide several play opportunities for toddlers.

1. Brush glue onto a paper plate and then help toddlers glue on little balls of scrunched-up tissue paper.

2. Put red around the edge, then orange, yellow, green, blue and purple. Cut the plate in half to make two rainbows.

Let toddlers draw on a plate with non-toxic wax crayons; they can eat a dry snack from it, afterwards.

String loop

Draw, or glue on mouths, noses and eyes for paper-plate faces. Glue on yarn for hair. Use string or yarn to hang the face up.

Help toddlers to make models of houses and buildings from food packaging and clear tape.

Packaging can be turned into all kinds of vehicles such as cars, trucks and space rockets.

Activities like this are ideal for several toddlers to do together.

- *Choose stories without too many words. Toddlers won't enjoy a story if it is too complex for them to understand.*

- *Stories about things that are familiar to toddlers, such as teddy bears or other children, are good places to start.*

- *Unusual ideas, such as toys going up in rockets, also appeal, as long as the language isn't too difficult.*

- *Stories with repetition are ideal, such as when the wolf 'huffs and puffs and blows the house down,' as toddlers soon learn to join in with these parts.*

- *Books with liftable flaps, tabs or pop-ups built into them are good, as they help children to feel involved in the story.*

Story time

At this stage, a toddler's language development can be truly amazing. Many toddlers who only knew a few words at 18 months can have a vocabulary of up to 200 words by the time they are two. Sharing stories can help make the most of a toddler's love of language.

Stories on tapes or CDs can help toddlers develop listening skills, improve concentration and provide an ideal break from active play. Try recording yourself reading some of a toddler's favorite stories. They won't mind if you don't sound like a professional.

Hearing a story lets toddlers imagine pictures to go with it, as they listen.

Sharing stories

Although most toddlers at this age still enjoy picture books, and will spend time turning the pages, most really enjoy listening to stories. Choosing the right story for a toddler can be tricky, but, as a general rule, you will know whether a book is at the right language level, or is interesting enough, if the child sits still long enough to listen to it. On the left are some more specific tips for finding good stories.

Although toddlers can't read, many enjoy looking at the pages of books on their own.

Tell me a story

Although toddlers love familiar stories, many demand new ones, freshly made-up just for them. If you don't find inventing stories easy, try basing them around the everyday events of a toddler's life. It's all gripping stuff to them.

Useful tip
It's unwise to try skipping a page, or shortening a favorite story; toddlers usually insist you read every word, every time...

Story sessions in libraries are a good way for toddlers to practice sitting and listening.

1. Draw a basic figure onto thin cardboard. Let the toddler scribble on some color with crayons before you cut the puppet out.

Cardboard loop

- The story of the toddler's day is always different. 'Then Jo ate pasta and an apple for lunch,' is simple, but important to that child.

- A photograph of the toddler can also provide a starting point for a story. You could say 'One day, Ben went to the beach,' for instance.

- Use a favorite toy as the focus in a story. Saying 'Teddy decided to go for a walk.' as you 'walk' the toy across your lap, is fine.

- It helps if some phrases always form part of your made-up stories. The ending 'then it was time for bed' will become reassuringly familiar.

2. Tape a loop of cardboard to the back of the puppet. Slide it onto the child's fingers and show them how to make it move, and 'talk.'

Toddlers enjoy making their toys act out 'stories', or everyday situations, as they play. Studies show that this kind of play is vital in helping children understand things that happen in their lives. Making simple finger puppets, as explained on the right, creates new characters for toddlers to include in their make-believe play.

3. If you make another puppet, the toddler can have one on each hand, or you can have one each to talk to each other in games.

- Don't invite too many children, and ask some adults to stay. Lots of toddlers need lots of attention.

- If you're going to serve food, do so near a mealtime to avoid tired, hungry toddlers.

- After food, an action-rhyme session might work well. Keep drinks available all the time.

- Consider renting a mini inflatable castle. Set up a quiet corner with crayons, too.

- Set up a cut and paste session at home for the birthday child and a few friends.

- In nice weather, you could meet friends for a picnic. Take the cake, outdoor toys, and a big blanket, and let the toddlers play.

- Try a trip to a zoo, an open farm or soft play center for a small group. Make sure enough grown-ups come too.

The second birthday

By the time a child is two, they will appreciate a party more than last year, but there's still no need to go all out. Two-year olds are too young for most party games, and are easily over-excited. Keep things simple, so that you can both enjoy the big day. If you decide to hold a party, there are a few guidelines to help you plan it on the left. It's a good idea to keep the sweet food hidden until the more healthy stuff has been eaten.

This time around, toddlers will probably be able to blow out the candles all by themselves.

Let's celebrate

Two-year olds may not understand much about birthdays, but they will know that they are the center of attention and most would prefer you to do the 'Hokey Pokey' with them than get stressed about sandwich fillings. A party with a few games, songs, some snacks and a cake with candles are a simple, traditional birthday celebration, but on the left are three more ideas to think about if you want to do something a little different.

Now they are two

Most toddlers change enormously during the six months after their second birthday. Some enter the busy, noisy world of a preschool or a playgroup for the first time. Many others become an older brother or sister, as a new baby arrives in the family. This is the last stage in this book and covers the age at which a child's unique personality really starts to assert itself.

How will my toddler change?

Their language develops rapidly. They will ask lots of questions and demand satisfying answers.

Most toddlers will use the potty and may be fully toilet-trained by two and a half. They can wash their hands too.

Toddlers can walk short distances alongside you. They are becoming more independent in all they do.

It may become clear whether a child is right- or left-handed now. They will use their 'preferred' hand most.

Many will be able to use silverware, and thread beads.

They can hold a crayon, or paintbrush, and draw lines with some control.

• Make sure you both wash your hands before you begin any cooking.

• Tell them that the oven is very hot. Keep them well away from it.

• Never leave them unsupervised. Accidents can only take a second.

• Keep any dangerous kitchen equipment well out of reach.

Toddler cooks

Cooking with a toddler may sound a little stressful, but, if you choose activities that suit the child's age and abilities, they'll really enjoy stirring, squirting and squeezing things in the kitchen with you – but be prepared for some mess! Most toddlers love cooking, but kitchens can be dangerous places, so they need to know that there are rules to follow. Stick to the guidelines on the left whenever you cook.

Roll, cut and stir

For a toddler, the best things about cooking are probably handling the food, and eating the results. This activity lets them do both:

1. Give a toddler some dough or pastry (store-bought is fine), and help them to roll it out.

2. Show them how to press shaped cutters into it, and lay the 'cookies' on a tray.

3. When they are cooked and cool, let them sprinkle on powdered sugar, or spread on some icing.

• When stirring a cake mixture or sauce, let them have a turn with the spoon.

• Let them stir some grated cheese into their pasta before eating it.

• Try letting toddlers stir some chopped fruit or a spoonful of honey into their yogurt.

For toddlers, feeling they are using the right cooking ingredients, as you do, is great.

Toddlers at this age will probably still enjoy stirring dried pasta in a pan or bowl, but they will be happier stirring something they can eat. On the left are three ways of helping toddlers feel involved in some 'real' cooking.

Toddler chefs

Lots of equipment isn't vital, but smaller rolling pins and wooden spoons do make things easier for toddler cooks. Putting on a special apron and covering or tying back their hair, as cooks do, makes the occasion more special. Let the 'chef' show everyone the finished product. Their sense of achievement will boost their confidence, and even if their efforts aren't perfect, it's important to praise them.

Making healthy food appealing to toddlers is not always easy. On the right are some ideas for involving a child in preparing the food, which often makes them happier to eat it.

• Provide a pizza crust, some sauce and assorted toppings in bowls. Help toddlers spoon on sauce, then add whatever they wish on top.

• Plain, oatmeal squares may not be popular, but if you let them sprinkle on some chopped, dried apricots or raisins, they may be.

• You might find chopped fresh fruit will be more popular if a toddler can spoon some low-fat yogurt on top.

Toddlers may have seen you doing things in the kitchen that they are eager to try themselves.

They will not mind that there's no hot water in their pan of pasta — it's the stirring they enjoy.

Using knives

Sharp kitchen knives are not suitable for toddlers, but, with careful supervision, they can learn how to cut with plastic ones, or blunt table knives. Let them try out their coordination on a peeled banana or a play-dough sausage.

As you cook and serve food, talk to toddlers about which foods are good, and which are not so good. This is how they'll learn healthy eating.

Drawing and coloring

There are few, simple, activities that absorb toddlers more than drawing. Learning how to hold crayons and make recognizable marks on paper takes some children longer than others, but the more practice they have, the more confident they will become.

Fingers and thumbs

Before about two-and-a-half years old, most toddlers hold a crayon with all their fingers and 'scrub' it across the page to make scribbly lines. Gradually, they learn what is called the tripod grip, which involves using their index and second fingers and their thumb to hold a crayon as they move it.

The best way to help children at this stage is to provide a choice of chunky crayons and chalks. As the months pass, add a few colored pencils and see how their fingers cope with them.

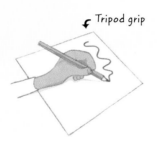

Toddlers need a lot of practice before they learn to control how a crayon makes marks on paper.

Tripod grip

Mastering the tripod grip will help children with their writing, later on, too.

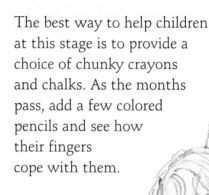

Toddlers may like drawing at an easel.

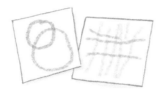

By two-and-a-half, toddlers may be able to draw circles, horizontal lines and 'V' shapes.

After a toddler's second birthday, you may notice them making more controlled lines and even circles, or copying simple 'V' or 'T' shapes. Their concentration will be immense, and many are upset if they feel they have gotten anything wrong. Let them keep trying, help them solve a problem if they seem stuck and remember to praise whatever they manage to produce.

Copy me

An ideal way of helping toddlers enjoy drawing is to show them that you enjoy it, too. Even if you doubt your artistic abilities, the simplest shape you draw will delight them. Try drawing a basic car or flower. (You could use a picture book for reference.) They may try to 'copy' your ideas, color them in, or just scribble all over them, but most toddlers will think drawing together is great.

Many toddlers want to draw themselves, or you. This is incredibly hard, and one way of fulfilling their desire to paint portraits may be to draw around peoples' hands or feet. On the right are some ideas to get you both started.

1. Ask them to put their hands, or feet, on some paper while you draw around them.

2. They can try to color in the outlines with crayons; don't worry if they can't do it neatly.

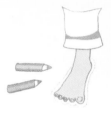

3. Let them draw around your hands or feet. Their lines may be wobbly, but they'll still have fun.

If you can, provide an art area for toddlers and encourage them to draw pictures there.

Online drawing

If you have access to a computer, toddlers as young as two usually enjoy on-screen drawing activities. They can learn how to use and control a mouse and how to choose and recognize colors and shapes in some art games. Displaying a print-out of the finished piece often goes over well. See page 118 for links to websites to try.

Useful tip
Don't let toddlers spend too long on the computer. Experts recommend that children spend no more than two hours a day in front of TV and computer screens.

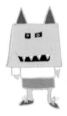

A box becomes a helmet or mask if you cut two holes in it. (Make sure they line up with the child's eyes).

Stick a box and a plastic cup or flowerpot onto a large box to make a castle tower. Cut a door for toddlers to open and shut.

An empty cardboard tube makes a good tunnel for toy cars. If it drops them into a box below, it's even better.

Make and build

Even the most active two-year-old will, eventually, get tired of racing around. Activities that give them the freedom to use their imagination, such as making or building something, can be ideal for these quieter times. It means that children are still busy, interested, and finding out new things as they play, but in their own way, and at their own pace.

Two-year-olds have many skills, and are adding to them every day. If you give them a variety of materials, you may be surprised at what they can do or make with them. Try letting the child enjoy what some experts call 'free-flow play'. This freedom to choose how to play is how children learn to make decisions, try out their ideas and to think.

Boxes and bottles

Empty cardboard boxes and clean plastic bottles give a toddler a chance to make things on a large scale. Let them experiment in how things fit together, helping them to glue, fold and tape if needed. There are some ideas for things to make on the left. Encourage them to tell you about whatever they have made, but be accepting if they don't want to.

Safety point

Never allow children to play with plastic bags, or put them anywhere near their heads or mouths.

Toddlers often have a very clear idea of what they are making — even if it's less clear to you.

Building blocks

A set of building blocks is a toy you can add to as a child grows and develops. Some kinds can be slotted or fitted together, for the toddler to make into countless different shapes and structures. If a toddler has run out of inspiration on their own, here are some ideas to try with blocks:

• Encourage them to see just how high a tower can go before it topples over. Count the bricks with them as they build upward.

• Make something from just green blocks together, then suggest the toddler makes something red, or blue. Let them tell you about it.

• Sit next to the child and help them to lay a ring of blocks all the way around both of you, to make a den.

• Encourage them to follow a trail of blocks that you lay for them. Now can they lay a trail for you?

Blocks that slot together are ideal for building tall towers, because they won't topple over.

Dough modeling

By this age, toddlers may be interested in doing more with play dough than just pummeling it. Let them find out what they can do and make with it. Once they have made what they want to, try these ideas together. Work alongside the child, helping if they ask you to, but letting them decide what goes where.

Make a dough spider. Roll a ball body and count the eight legs as you roll them out and stick them on.

Roll out dough sausages and tiny peas. Flatten some dough and use a plastic knife to cut some fries.

Try making a long, thin sausage snake and giving it two eyes. Add a wiggle in the body if you wish.

Ask toddlers to copy what you do. Make some of your actions energetic, and others less so, to make sure they watch you carefully.

Rough and tumble games can really help toddlers' physical confidence. Hold their legs as a wheelbarrow, wrestle or give them a piggyback ride.

Most toddlers swerve to avoid things rather than bump into them now. Set up obstacles, such as chairs, and let them race around them.

Safety point

At times, toddlers get small bumps and bruises during play. Try to accept it, comfort them, but don't stop them from playing.

Fun and games

Young children learn just as much from physical play as they do from books and toys. By two years old, they can run, jump and climb and are full of energy, so it's more important than ever to give them regular, active play.

In the past, some experts believed that physical play was not essential for young children, but simply a break from 'real' learning. Studies now show that children really need opportunities to take part in energetic play if they are to develop into healthy, happy adults.

Active games help improve a toddler's coordination.

All together

One of the best things about active play is that children can enjoy it with others, too. Toddlers often play simple versions of tag and hide-and-seek, run and explore outside or build dens together. Playing like this helps them learn to make decisions, solve problems and cooperate. They may still prefer to play alone most of the time, but the more chances they have to play with others, the better.

Move to the music

Experts have found that toddlers instinctively move their bodies when they hear music. They seem programmed to respond to it, which makes it an ideal way to get them moving. The three ideas on the right work inside, and may encourage more reluctant movers to take part, too.

Toddlers are very flexible and can stretch and move far more easily than adults.

• Move to some music together, then turn it off and stay still. When you turn the music on again, both start moving.

• Put on some music with a strong beat or with changes of mood in it. Encourage the toddler to dance to it however they want to.

• Action songs encourage physical coordination. Songs such as 'If you're happy and you know it' work well, for example.

Water work-out

Moving in water is excellent exercise, so regular trips to a swimming pool are a good idea. You could try doing some action rhymes, such as 'Ring Around the Rosies', in shallow water with them. On the right are two more pre-swimming ideas for two-year-olds, which will help build their confidence. Make sure you supervise them all the time, even if they are using a flotation aid, and don't stay in the pool for any longer than 40 minutes at a time.

Foam noodle

By this stage, toddlers can use a foam noodle in the water. Make sure they don't let go.

Practicing blowing a small ball across the water, will help them to control their breathing.

Who shall I be?

After their second birthday, most children begin to play games that involve some make-believe. This kind of play helps toddlers learn about how to express and control their emotions, and how other people behave and feel. It's particularly important for their social development, too, as they start to play with other children.

1. To make a hat you need a thin sheet of cardboard, some tape and some gold stars.

Trim off excess

2. Roll the sheet of cardboard into a pointed cone and tape it together.

3. Decorate the hat by sticking on the gold stars (or other shapes).

Role-playing

Encourage toddlers to play freely and try not to steer boys away from traditional 'female' roles, or the other way around. In today's society, men need to cook and change diapers and women need to change fuses and use drills, so, if you can, try to avoid giving children the impression that roles for men and women are clear cut.

Toddlers will be all the happier to take on a role if they have been involved in making a costume. Let them decorate crowns or paint a cardboard shield. On the left there's a basic hat design you could adapt in many different ways.

Toddlers' make-believe games often center around small toys, as they invent 'mini-worlds' for them.

For them, their toys are very real, with feelings and personalities of their own.

How to help

Toddlers don't usually need much help to invent make-believe games. There's still no need to buy expensive costumes, but a few props will probably go over well and make it all the more fun for them.

A toy doctor's kit provides endless chances to make Teddy better...

- A collection of hats, helmets, bags, boots, belts or fabric cloaks opens a world of roles.

- A strip of cloth makes an ideal bandage for Teddy's sore paw, or head.

- Big boxes can become houses or caves to hide in, or cars to ride in. Smaller ones make beds for toys.

Face painting

Few two-year-olds will stay still long enough for an elaborate face-painting session, but you can really add to their make-believe fun with some simple face-painting techniques. Here are a few useful tips to help you get started:

- Make sure your hands and the child's face are clean and dry before you start.

- Use water-based face paints and make sure both of you wear old clothes.

- Makeup sponges work well for applying the face paints. Use a fine brush for detail.

- Let the toddler try. Just before bathtime might be an ideal time...

Toddlers love seeing themselves transformed with face paints.

Let's get wet!

1. Tell the child you're going out together, and that it's raining outside. Can the toddler go and find their raincoat and boots?

2. Put your wet weather gear on together, showing them how to tuck pants into boots, and do up their coats as well.

3. If you have umbrellas, put them up outside your door. This still leaves you with a hand free to hold the child's hand.

4. Lift your faces to the rain. Join the toddler in stomping in puddles and watching where the water goes.

5. Explain how flowers, trees, animals and people need rainwater. At home, take wet clothes off and warm up quickly.

Safety point

It's important to supervise young children at all times when they are playing with water.

Strange as it may sound, it's a good idea to let toddlers get wet regularly. Having confidence in and around water is essential, and so is an awareness of its dangers, but water play needn't always mean trips to the swimming pool. On these pages there are some simple ideas that should help even reluctant toddlers see that getting wet can be fun.

Few people like getting soaked, but, if you are wearing waterproof clothes and boots and it's not too cold or lightning, going for a walk on a rainy day can be an enjoyable experience for a young child. Find out how to make the best of rainy trips with the tips on the left.

For little children, there's nothing quite like splashing in puddles.

What lives in water?

Young children are fascinated by animals, including those that live in water. Having your own pond can bring its own worries, unless you are with the toddler at all times, but visits to aquariums, pet stores and ponds in parks are all valuable. Even a few minutes spent at a store selling fresh fish gives you the chance to tell toddlers that some creatures can breathe in water… but people can't.

Fearful faces

Some toddlers don't like getting their faces wet, which can make bathtime, and swimming trips, difficult. It may help if you make bathtimes as splashy as possible. Encourage the toddler to dunk their bath toys underwater, wash them with sponges or just pour some water over them. On the right are some more ways of tackling this fear and increasing a child's confidence.

Toddler toy wash

If the weather is warm, try lining up a toddler's waterproof toys outside ready to be washed in a 'toy wash'. Most toddlers enjoy sponging and rinsing their trucks and trikes.

Many toddlers will be just as happy to spend time playing with small toys in a sink, or a bowl full of water, as they were when they were younger. They may now invent make-believe games with boats or ducks, but a selection of plastic containers will still give them plenty of play opportunities. It's a good idea to spread out some newspaper or a plastic tablecloth first.

Being allowed to find out what water does may absorb toddlers for ages.

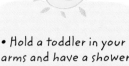

• *Hold a toddler in your arms and have a shower together. Let them see you close your eyes and let the water run over your face.*

• *Outside, sprinklers and hoses can be fun. Even nervous toddlers usually can't resist creeping near the jet of water.*

• *Throw water-filled balloons outdoors. They can make getting wet so much fun, it may not seem as scary.*

1. Stand opposite the toddler and gently throw, roll, or kick a ball toward them.

2. If things go well, both take a step back after each successful catch or kick.

3. Try some higher and lower throws, then get them to dribble the ball to you.

4. If they grab the ball and run, they may have had enough. Just relax and chase them.

Useful tip

Take a toddler to play in a ball pit, if a local family entertainment center has one. There, they can throw, kick and catch thousands of balls.

Balls and beanbags

Balls are versatile toys, and most toddlers enjoy playing with them. By the age of two, they can usually kick and catch a large, soft ball successfully. It's worth buying a selection of different-sized balls, so children can choose the best one for kicking, catching, rolling or throwing. The games on these pages will help develop a toddler's strength, coordination, and physical skills.

Soccer balls are too hard and heavy for toddlers, but foam balls or blow-up beach balls are ideal. They are light and easy to grab.

Aim and throw

Toddlers can be powerful throwers, but find it hard to learn how to aim and throw things to each other or so that they land somewhere specific. Try standing close to a wastepaper basket with them and encourage the child to throw a ball or beanbag into it. Take a step back after every 'goal'. This activity demands concentration, so keep it fun.

Bowling

Aiming and rolling a ball so that it hits another object is no small feat for a young child, but they may master it and have fun playing simple versions of bowling games. Toddler bowling involves placing a ball in front of the child and showing them how to roll another ball so that they 'crash'. Try it down a hallway, moving back a little each time.

Half fill plastic bottles with play sand and replace the caps tightly to make pins.

Exercise balls

Although large, inflatable exercise balls are made for adults, toddlers can benefit from them if you help them use them properly. Let the child lie tummy-down across the ball, with their legs and arms spread out. Hold the ball steady. This stretches out lots of vital muscles. There are two more suggestions for ways of using them on the right.

• Exercise balls are great for stretching backs. Put the child on top, hold their hips and ask them to go floppy.

• If they feel confident, gently roll the ball to and fro with the toddler on top. This can relieve tummy pains.

Make your own beanbags

Beanbags often become favorite toys for toddlers, especially when made from furry or animal-print fabrics. All you need to make one is a rectangle of fabric, a sewing maching (or needle and thread) and some dried beans.

Safety point

Keep dried beans out of the reach of toddlers and check beanbags regularly for holes before you let children play with them.

1. Cut a piece of fabric 12 inches long and 6 inches wide.

2. Fold the fabric in half and double-stitch two of the open sides.

3. Hold the bag 'open side up' and fill it with dried beans.

4. Finally, sew the last side up securely to finish the beanbag.

- Stick to set times when they take a bath, their teeth and hair are brushed. Don't offer a choice — these things must happen.

- Let the toddler take a turn at brushing hair and teeth (after you've done them). This gives them some control, and teaches them how to do it.

- Introduce little games or routines. If musical tooth-brushes make things easier, that's fine. Hum as you brush, and praise their 'shiny teeth'.

- Many toddlers will be using the potty now (but aren't diaperless yet). You may do the bottom-wiping, but both of you can wash your hands.

More about me

Many toddlers have considerable willpower, definite likes and dislikes, and growing physical strength as well. By the age of two-and-a-half, they can recognize themselves in photos and mirrors, and may seem to talk and ask questions all the time. They are now little people in their own right.

Of course, most toddlers are far more interested in playing than in brushing their teeth, or taking a bath. Avoiding a clash of wills about things like this can be hard. Telling a child that they need to take care of their bodies can help, as can showing them that you have to do these things regularly too. There are some more tips on the left.

Listen to me

Young children really benefit from one-to-one attention from a familiar adult. You may find that building this into each day makes the difficult parts easier to cope with. As you sit on the sofa or walk to the park, try spending a while talking to them about things they see and do.

For toddlers, there are few things more fascinating than themselves.

I am this big...

Toddlers know what they look like in pictures, but these images are not life-size. You could make a mark of their height on a door frame or height chart from time to time, to show how they're growing. On the right is another way of showing their real size – and how big they've become.

Back of wallpaper

1. Unroll enough old wallpaper or lining paper on the floor for the toddler to lie down on it.

2. Ask the toddler to lie really still while you draw around them with a crayon or marker.

Toddlers often want to check 'who is the biggest' when playing with friends.

3. Cut the outline out and let them color in each part of their body with crayons.

4. Tape the outline to a wall and let the toddler stand next to it and 'measure up'.

Look how I've grown!

This activity is ideal for a quiet time together. It gives a toddler the chance to think about, and talk to you about, themselves, and how they are changing and growing.

• Bring out some recent photos of the toddler. Do they remember where the pictures were taken? Give them time to answer. Their memories may surprise you.

• If you have a box of photos, try putting together a sequence showing them as they grow up. Talk about how they've changed from their tiny baby days.

• You could glue the photos onto sheets of thin cardboard and put them in a ring binder. A few words about each one makes a 'Book about me'.

Useful tip

Laminating photos makes them more toddler-proof. Many copy centers have laminating machines.

All about animals

Although many toddlers might not have seen a real elephant or giraffe, most can recognize them right away in books, or on television. Animals are fascinating for small children, and they seem able to remember lots of things about them with ease. Games and activities based on animals can provide lots of opportunities for play.

Children know that animals are amazingly varied. They see that they can have spots, stripes, teeth, trunks, tails and tusks. They know they may bark, roar, purr, croak or hiss. Encourage this curiosity with the activities on the left

• Cut pictures of animals from magazines into two or three pieces. Ask the toddler to put the animals back together. Try mismatching pieces, too, to make new creatures.

• When looking at pictures of animals, encourage toddlers to make the right noise. If you get it wrong, and roar when you see a frog, they'll enjoy correcting you.

• Draw, trace or print out some simple outlines of animals for a toddler to identify and color in. Find some on the Usborne Quicklinks Website (see page 118).

Small toys, big games

Toy manufacturers know toddlers love animals, but you don't need to fill your home with huge, soft toys. Some small realistic animals will probably inspire all sorts of make-believe games. Toddlers often become absorbed in the needs of their animals, caring for them, or putting them into families. You could add to this collection when the toddler deserves a treat and make a game out of guessing which one you've bought, by giving 'noisy' clues before producing it...

Useful tip

Many toy stores sell CDs of animal noises. These encourage children to concentrate and listen as they try to identify them (as well as being fun).

Lots of toddlers go through a phase of wanting to collect things. For many, toy animals fit the bill perfectly.

'What am I?'

Toddlers are too young for complex role-play, but many enjoy pretending to be animals. Encourage them to move and sound like the animal they choose. There are many animal accessories available to buy to add to this kind of play, but there are tips for making your own on the right and on the Usborne Quicklinks Website (see page 118).

Some toddlers get so involved in pretending to be animals that the main problem can be getting them to stop...

• *Animal masks can be basic cardboard cut-outs or more lifelike versions. They add to a toddler's pretend play, but make sure they fit well.*

• *A selection of furry or felt ears sewn onto headbands and long or fluffy tails that can be clipped or pinned on to clothes may be popular.*

• *Dressing-up animal suits can be expensive. Often, basic face-paint spots and stripes will be enough.*

Animal magic

On a daily basis, the best way to encourage a toddler's interest in animals is to look at them in books or watch them on TV or wildlife DVDs. This may well become a child's favorite activity for a while. Many well-known children's stories have an animal as the star. As a toddler makes sense of the world, they seem to gain comfort from the gentle predictability of stories about a dog or penguin.

Teaching toddlers how to pet an animal gently, and treat it with care, is a good idea. This doesn't mean you need to own a pet, but try to let toddlers see and touch (friendly) live animals from time to time. A trip to a petting zoo is a big treat for a young child, or seeing that elephants and tigers are real at a wildlife park or zoo is incredibly exciting.

Taking care of friends' pets while they're away can give some experience of caring for animals.

• Lift up a stone to see who's living under it. Make sure toddlers treat what they find with care and put it back afterward.

• Look at the veins on the back of leaves. Lay paper over them and let the toddler scribble with a wax crayon to make a pattern.

• If you find a spider's web near home, sprinkle a little flour onto it to make the pattern of the web easier for a toddler to see.

• In spring, pick a twig with leaf buds on it and put it in some water. After a few days, the new leaves should start to unfurl.

• In the fall, search for brightly colored leaves. You could press some between two sheets of book covering film.

What's outside?

There are always different things for young children to look at, and find out about, outside. They have greater freedom to explore, make lots of noise and see something new when they are out in the open air, too. There are lots of suggestions for taking a first look at nature with a curious toddler on these two pages.

If you take young children into a park, or any open, green space, they will be intensely interested what they find there. There are all kinds of things you could look out for, from wiggly worms to cones, seeds and flowers. You can help encourage their interest further with some first science activities. The ideas on the left should help get you started.

Looking at flowers, leaves and bugs can keep a toddler busy for some time.

Wildlife and weather

Wildlife can be limited in some places, but birds live in even the most crowded of cities. You can introduce toddlers to the birds that live nearby by feeding them. If you have an outdoor space, try hanging bird feeders out. See which birds visit and what kind of food each one prefers.

By two-and-a-half, many toddlers have noticed that the weather is not always the same. They will have heard you say that they need to wear a coat as it's raining, or a sun hat on sunny days many times (though they may always not be willing to do so…). Try keeping a picture weather chart for a week, to increase their awareness of how each day is different.

Wrapping up and going for a walk gives a toddler the chance to experience the day's weather, not just see it from indoors.

Some bird feeders are designed to hang outside windows, or stick to the outside of them.

1. Draw, color and cut out simple paper suns, gray rain clouds, or white fluffy clouds. (Do other weather, such as snow, when needed.)

2. Write the days of the week on a basic chart. Help the toddler decide which weather picture to stick on. (Some days may need several…)

3. Talk about what they could do, and what they should wear, today. This helps them understand how the weather affects them.

Eggheads

Toddlers are often interested in how things grow, but may not have much patience to wait for it to happen. For this quick growing activity, you'll need a clean, empty hard-boiled eggshell, cotton balls and some cress seeds:

1. Be careful not to crush the bottom half of the shell, draw eyes, a mouth and nose on it.

2. Soak a cotton ball in water and put it carefully into the bottom of the shell.

3. Sprinkle on some cress seeds. Keep the cotton moist until the seeds sprout.

4. Within days, cress 'hair' will grow. Snip it with scissors and use it in some sandwiches.

What shall we do today?

Entertaining and educating a toddler can be great fun, but it can also be challenging to meet all their needs day after day. There are some coping tactics on this page, plus some ideas to help you survive the days when you have nothing planned, it's only 8:00am, and bedtime seems a long way away...

As a general rule, it's a good idea to try to follow a basic daily routine with a toddler. Research shows that toddlers feel happier, and safer, if they know what to expect, so structuring your days to some degree may help you both.

- If you do something energetic in the morning, plan a quieter activity for after lunch. If a child still naps, build that into your plans, too.

- Snuggling up and watching a suitable TV program or DVD with a child is fine. It gives you both time to relax, and recharge your batteries.

- Meals split up the day naturally. If you can, try to keep to fairly regular mealtimes, as tired, hungry toddlers are harder to amuse.

Making friends

It's important for both of you to get out and meet other people, so make the effort to go to a local toddlers' group. Many two-and-a-half-year olds still find it hard to play with other children, but their social skills will only improve if they are given chances to practice. Many toddlers' groups have drink and snack time, clean-up time, and singing or stories to end with. It's good for toddlers to see that other places have rules and routines.

Useful tip
Try to remember that, although days at home might feel a bit dull to you, for toddlers, every day is different, and full of new things to do.

Toddlers' groups give a toddler the chance to play with new toys and other children.

Me and you

Two-year-olds are still very dependent on whoever is caring for them, and prefer to have your full attention. This is natural – but tiring, and unrealistic when you have other things to do, too. Try varying the activities you do with a toddler, so that you do some things together and others alongside each other.

If you're busy in the kitchen, let toddlers 'help' you, by washing plastic cups, bowls and spoons.

Regular routines are good, but it's fine if some days are different. Don't worry if a toddler has to eat a sandwich in the car, or skip a bath one night as you've been out for a long day together. As long as you are relaxed about changes in routine, toddlers are likely to be as well, and some of the best fun, and best memories, are the result of experiences which may have been unplanned.

Just the two of us

Today, in our busy lives, it can seem hard to find the hours in the day to do all the things you need to do – at home, at work, for a child, let alone for yourself. Recent research shows how important it is simply to try to give children some of your time. The vacuuming will wait: half an hour spent chatting with you about the day's events, or things that matter to them, may mean far more to a small child than you realize.

Playing with you...

• Play the 'mirror' game, where the toddler stands opposite you and tries to copy exactly what you do.

• When there's no hurry, go for a walk at their pace. They will enjoy showing you things that interest them.

• Sit down somewhere comfortable with a few favorite books and read or talk about them together.

Playing beside you...

• While you are sorting out the laundry, see if they can fold up all of their own or their toys' clothes neatly.

• If you have things to do outside, let toddlers water the flowers with a mini-watering can.

• While you are cooking, set them up at a table with some chunky wax crayons and a sheet of paper.

A quiet chat and cuddle is always reassuring for a toddler.

- Build up a social life for a toddler. If you can, take them to see friends and family regularly, and talk about them after visits.

- Look at photos of the important people in their lives. Encourage them to say their names when they recognize them.

- Include babysitters, nannies or other caregivers in your chats about people. Talk about what toddlers do when they are with them.

- Stick some photos onto a simple chart, and write peoples' names under them. A child may want to display it on the wall.

Toddlers feel a huge range of emotions, and need practice to learn how to control them.

It's my world

In a toddler's mind, everyone else is around mainly to meet their needs. This is perfectly natural at this stage of their development, and partly true, after all; they are at the heart of a network of family and friends who care for them.

As a child's emotional awareness grows, it's important to talk about, and celebrate the fact that they have people in their lives that are 'precious' to them. It helps them feel secure, and establishes their sense of who they are. Between the ages of two and three, they'll begin to be more aware of others' needs and feelings. You can help increase this, and their self-confidence, with activities such as those on the left.

Talking about the important people in a child's life can help them to feel secure.

Show and tell

It's healthy for everyone involved to openly discuss feelings. If a child shows you they are sad, saying 'I can see that you're sad' can help them understand, and cope with it better. Toddlers will learn to manage their feelings, but need to know that hitting or kicking when they're angry is wrong, for instance. There are rules to be followed, and you need to set them. It's good to show how you feel, too. Say: 'You've made me feel upset', and explain why. Toddlers need to learn that their actions may have consequences – both good and bad.

How do you feel?

Toddlers show you how they are feeling in three main ways. They may tell you, show you in their behavior or their body language, or reveal feelings as they play. Watch a child closely to learn more about how they are feeling. Try setting up play that needs them to focus on how people, or toys, might feel in different situations:

• Let them bathe their dolls or put their toys to bed. If one of them is 'sick', it gives a toddler the chance to 'make them better'.

• Set up a toys' tea party with real food, and let a toddler feed them. It may be interesting to see which toy gets the best food.

• Don't panic if they're harsh with toys, or punish them. It's natural, and better, for them to act out such feelings in play, not reality.

A toddler's behavior and body language can tell you a lot about how they are feeling.

Strong feelings

For a toddler, the world is a very emotional place, and they have not learned to hide or control their feelings yet. They will most likely cry, laugh, shout, shriek and feel real fury every single day. If they can't make themselves understood, or do something they want to do, they will rage with frustration.

Most adults find toddlers' behavior hard to deal with at times. Try to be patient, and keep calm. They don't mean to anger or embarrass you, and need your love above all. Their worries and fears are painfully real. If you can, grit your teeth, breathe deeply, count to ten, distract, or just ignore them if they are misbehaving.

For toddlers, every day is an emotional rollercoaster, but their bad moods rarely last long.

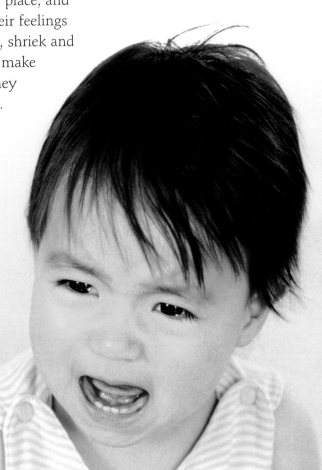

• Before you leave home, put a drink, snack, book and some small toys into a bag.

• Bring these offerings out one at a time, with plenty of smiles and enthusiastic 'oohs'.

• Make sure there is always a notebook and box of small crayons in the bag.

• If all else fails, let a toddler just delve in... but watch what they put in their mouths.

Small board books and toys that fit together are great basics for a going-out bag.

What to do when

The ideas on these two pages are practical tips for entertaining a toddler in situations which can be difficult, such as long journeys in a car, long stints in a waiting room or eating out in a café or restaurant when toddlers can be restless, and hard to amuse.

Look what's in my bag...

A long wait in the doctor's waiting room is frustrating for anyone, but for toddlers, who are easily bored, it's even more so. A bag kept for outings could be the solution. On the left are some ideas for what you could put in it, but, whatever you choose, remember to change the contents regularly so the toddler doesn't get bored with them.

Doctors, dentists, banks and other offices often keep a few toys for visiting toddlers. Try asking if you forget your own.

Eating out

It's a treat to eat in a café, or a restaurant sometimes. Toddlers remember experiences like this, but they can also be a flashpoint for bad behavior. On the right are some guidelines for avoiding a stressful time, but try not to get too upset if a toddler does misbehave in public. Most people will sympathize – and you can only do your best.

If toddlers are bored, they are more likely to misbehave. Give them plenty to keep them busy.

• See if the restaurant is child-friendly. Does it have highchairs, a child's menu, and other children eating in it?

• Before you order, try to find out how long the food will be. A long wait to eat can spell disaster with toddlers.

• Prepare your going-out bag with essentials (ex. a favorite picture book, notepad, crayons, your key ring).

• If a toddler gets fed up, take them out of the highchair for a walk, exploring the café. This distraction may help.

Back-seat driver

Taking a toddler in the car can be an enjoyable experience for both of you. They may happily chat away, pointing at diggers or cows they see. For longer trips, however, it's a good idea to have some survival strategies. Try these:

• Stop every hour or so, for them to move around for a few minutes and get some fresh air.

• Keep a selection of nursery rhyme and song tapes or CDs in the car to sing along to.

• Give them a toddler-safe, wipe-clean drawing board with a pen that's attached.

• Small, healthy snacks and a drink will help to break up the journey time.

Keep an interesting toy, such as a baby steering wheel or an activity center, in the car, as something to look forward to.

1. *Out of the toddler's view, put a little toddler-friendly food, such as cereal, cheese cubes and chopped fruit into plastic bowls.*

2. *Put a hand over the toddler's eyes and let them taste each food and tell you what it is. (Beware: this may get messy...)*

3. *Now let them cover your eyes, and watch you taste and guess which food is which. If you make a 'deliberate mistake', all the better.*

Rainy day ideas

These activities are designed to give a toddler a new experience without your having to spend any money or go out. They are probably best saved for a rainy afternoon, when you have time, but little energy.

The ideas on the left use everyday objects to help develop a toddler's sensory awareness, as they touch and taste things. They'll improve their verbal skills too, as they tell you all about it.

Bubble fun

Most toddlers enjoy racing around, trying to catch and pop bubbles. Bottles of ready-made bubble solution are cheap, but when the solution runs out, or gets spilled, try refilling the bottle with 90% cold water and 10% dishwashing liquid. Some toy stores also sell giant bubble-blowing trays. These bring enormous pleasure (and produce enormous bubbles) without your having to spend a fortune.

1. *Put a selection of toys and safe, everyday objects such as sieves or spoons into a cloth sack or pillowcase.*

2. *Try to choose objects of varying textures and shapes. Can they guess what each one is through the cloth?*

3. *Let the toddler enjoy the surprise of seeing whether they guessed correctly when they pull each item out.*

Bubble-blowing works well indoors or outside.

Useful information

In this part of the book, you'll find information that is useful to know as a parent or caregiver. Use it as a starting point, as there's a huge amount of information available on the internet and in other books, magazines and leaflets for, and about, babies and toddlers and their needs and development.

What will I find here?

Basic first-aid advice for everyday children's ailments and minor accidents.

Guidelines for caring for children with special needs, and sources of support.

Songs and action rhymes that are usually popular with babies and toddlers.

Information about child development and what to look for at each stage.

Information about useful websites to visit.

Special needs

This book cannot give in-depth information about caring for babies and toddlers with special needs, but many of the activities in it can be enjoyed by all kinds of children. Here are some general approaches to use when entertaining and educating children with special needs.

Count me in

Today, most experts believe that parents and other caregivers should let children with special needs try things alongside other children as much as possible and that this benefits all the children involved. This 'can do' approach, which concentrates on each child having the same experiences as everyone else, is called inclusion. Of course, if any child with special needs becomes frustrated or distressed during a play activity, help them, or leave the activity for another day, just as you would for any child.

It's vital to plan a play activity carefully. Are the toys easily reachable from a wheelchair? If a child cannot see well, choose an activity that gives them the chance to touch, or smell, for example.

Below are a few other things to think about to try to ensure that children with special needs are included in all play activities.

• Often, small adaptations make all the difference. Putting toys on a non-slip mat means they are less likely to fall or roll out of a less mobile toddler's reach.

• Try to see things from the child's point of view. Being left on the edge of the room is lonely. Let wheelchair users be in the middle of things as much as possible.

• Remember all babies and toddlers need a variety of things to play with, look at and do. Some can't tell you they're bored by crawling off, or choosing another toy.

• There's no need to spend huge amounts on specially adapted toys. Children enjoy some aspects of most toys. Variety, and understanding their needs, is the key.

Be aware of...

Different children have different needs, but here are some things to bear in mind when setting up play opportunities for children with specific disabilities:

Children with Down's syndrome

Children with Down's are often very sociable and enjoy playing with other children, but you may need to bear hearing and sight impairments in mind. As their development may be slower, let them play with the toys they choose, at their own pace.

Children with learning disabilities

Children can have a range of learning disabilities, and each may need a different approach. Patience, reassurance and consistency are vital for all of them. Be clear in what you expect of the child, and offer them varied, interesting play opportunities.

Children with hearing impairment

Children who cannot hear perfectly may find being in a busy, noisy toddlers' group stressful. Make sure they don't feel isolated. They may particularly enjoy toys with lights, hums or vibrations, interesting textures or different scents.

It's important for toddlers to learn to be considerate of another child's needs, whatever they may be.

Children with sight impairment

These children may need a little help as they move around a new play space. Offer them toys they can get to know through touch and sound. Ones with different shapes, textures and noises are ideal, as are bold, bright colors and strong patterns.

Children with limited mobility

Children who use a wheelchair, or have limited mobility, may need help to get where they want to play. Offer them toys that are solidly made, with buttons and levers that are easy to use. Toys such as activity centers should, ideally, have non-slip bases.

Walking frames are available for even the smallest of children.

Children on the autistic spectrum

For these children, too much noise and activity can be hard to cope with, as can sudden changes of routine. Toys and activities that give them the chance to discover things for themselves and a calm, orderly play space are important.

Getting support

Caring for children with special needs is a very demanding job. There are many organizations and groups that offer support, and ideas for play activities that help all kinds of children's physical and emotional development, so you need not feel alone. Ask your healthcare professionals if you are feeling unsure where to look for help. See page 118 for links to websites which may be useful to you, too.

Everyday ailments

Young children are incredibly active, and largely fearless, so it is likely that they are going to have some tumbles, and feel unwell, from time to time. Here's how to deal with everyday, minor accidents and some common childhood illnesses.

Minor cuts and scrapes

Toddlers are particularly prone to cuts and scrapes. If the wound is on the head, or will not stop bleeding, you need to get medical help immediately.

1. Comfort the toddler, wash your hands, and sit them down comfortably.

2. Gently wash the cut under running water, or dab it with an alcohol-free wipe. When it's dry, cover with some sterile gauze.

3. If you can, raise the injured area a little and clean around it. If the wound is still bleeding, press on it firmly.

4. Remove the gauze and cover the wound with a dressing or adhesive bandage bigger than the cut itself.

Decorated bandages can console a toddler, but some children are allergic to bandages and need dressings instead.

Burns and scalds

Remember that babies and toddlers have delicate skin. They can even be burned by radiators and hot pipes.

1. Take a burned or scalded child away from the problem. Hold wherever is burned under cold running water for at least 10 minutes.

2. Take any clothes around the area off, cutting them if necessary, but don't try to remove fabric stuck to the burned or scalded skin.

3. Once cool, cover the area with a loose sterile dressing. Call an ambulance or take the child to the hospital.

Bumps and bruises

Unfortunately, toddlers often fall and bump themselves as they play and explore. Usually, a cuddle, gently raising the hurt area and keeping a cool, wet towel on it for five minutes will be enough to 'make it better'. If a child has hit their head, however, you need to keep a close eye on them for the next 24 hours. If they become very drowsy, are sick, or say they can't see properly, take them straight to the hospital, as they may have a concussion.

Rashes

Babies and toddlers can often have diaper rash (which is treatable with creams), heat rash (for which cold water is best), or patches of eczema (which a doctor can prescribe cream for). If a baby or toddler seems very sick, and has purply spots that do not become paler if you press a glass gently over them, take the child to the hospital immediately. These can be signs of the illness meningitis.

Choking

If a baby or toddler is choking, something is stuck in their throat, they can't breathe in and may turn blue from lack of oxygen. If they can't cough the object out, you need to act fast. Stay calm, and follow these steps.

Babies under one year old

1. Lay the baby face down across your lap, or along your forearm. Make sure their head is lower than their body.

2. Give up to five sharp blows with the heel of your hand. Check their mouth after each blow.

3. If the baby is still choking, place two fingers a finger's width below the line of their nipples and push up to five times on their breastbone.

4. Check their mouth after each thrust. If it is not clear, get medical help.

Babies and toddlers over a year old

1. For toddlers, stand or kneel behind them and wrap both your arms around the top half of their body.

2. Place one of your fists between their belly button and the bottom of their breastbone, between their ribs, and hold on to it with your other hand.

3. Pull the fist upward and inward sharply up to five times, but do not use too much force.

4. Check the child's mouth after each thrust. If it is not clear, get medical help. Always take a toddler who has had abdominal thrusts to a doctor to be checked afterward.

Something's stuck

Babies and toddlers may put small things in ears, noses, or up their bottoms, where they can get stuck. If you can't easily remove the object, take the child to a hospital, to get such things out safely.

Sunburn

Young children burn quickly in hot sun and should, ideally, always be kept in the shade. Make sure you use a children's sunscreen and put a hat on a child if in the sun. If skin is red and sore after sun-exposure, follow these steps.

1. Cool their skin with a sponge and cold water, or put the sore area in a cold bath for 10 minutes.

2. If the doctor advises, gently apply aloe-vera or calamine lotion.

3. Give the child a cold drink and take off any hot clothes.

4. If the skin blisters, take the child to the doctor.

Sun hats that shade the back of a child's neck as well as the whole face are ideal.

Fever

A baby or child with a high temperature will be hot and possibly clammy to the touch, probably miserable, and may have a blank look in their eyes.

1. Take the child's temperature with a thermometer. A normal temperature is 97–99°F.

2. If it is too high, give them some acetaminophen. Be sure to consult the doctor for children under 6 months old. Take off their clothes and put the child somewhere cool, with plenty of cool drinks.

3. Try sponging their body with washcloths dipped in tepid water and squeezed out. If you are at all concerned, take the child to the doctor.

Songs and rhymes

Here are some well-known songs and rhymes that are fun to
share with babies and toddlers. It's best to leave some of the
more boisterous action rhymes until babies can hold their
heads up confidently, as too much bouncing could hurt them.

Nursery rhymes

Most babies and toddlers love having traditional rhymes sung to
them. They'll become a part of their childhood, something they
remember fondly, as you probably do from when you were small.

Little Bo-Peep

Little Bo-Peep has lost her sheep,
And doesn't know where to find them;
Leave them alone, and they'll come home,
Wagging their tails behind them.

Baa, baa, black sheep

Baa, baa, black sheep,
Have you any wool?
Yes sir, yes sir,
Three bags full:
One for the master,
And one for the dame,
And one for the little boy
Who lives down the lane.

Jack and Jill

Jack and Jill went up the hill,
To fetch a pail of water;
Jack fell down and broke his crown,
And Jill came tumbling after.

Up Jack got, and home did trot,
As fast as he could caper;
He went to bed to mend his head,
With vinegar and brown paper.

Humpty Dumpty

Humpty Dumpty sat on a wall,
Humpty Dumpty had a great fall;
All the king's horses and all the king's men
Couldn't put Humpty together again.

Hey diddle diddle

Hey diddle diddle,
The cat and the fiddle,
The cow jumped over the moon;
The little dog laughed
To see such fun,
And the dish ran away with the spoon.

Hickory, dickory, dock

Hickory, dickory, dock!
The mouse ran up the clock;
The clock struck one,
The mouse ran down,
Hickory, dickory dock!

Mary had a little lamb

Mary had a little lamb,
Its fleece was white as snow,
And everywhere that Mary went,
The lamb was sure to go.

Counting rhymes

These rhymes are a fun, easy way to introduce numbers and counting to babies and toddlers. As they learn the words through lots of repetition, they learn the numbers too.

One potato, two potato

One potato, two potato,
Three potato, four,
Five potato, six potato,
Seven potato, more!

One two, three, four, five

One two, three, four, five,
Once I caught a fish alive;
Six, seven, eight, nine, ten,
Then I let it go again.

Lullabies

Babies all over the world have been soothed to sleep by lullabies.
These three are ideal for bedtime, and, over time, most babies
begin to associate hearing them with falling asleep.

Rock-a-bye baby

Rock-a-bye baby, on the tree top,
When the wind blows, the cradle will rock.
When the bough breaks, the cradle will fall,
And down will come baby, cradle and all.

Twinkle, twinkle, little star

Twinkle, twinkle, little star,
How I wonder what you are,
Up above the world so high,
Like a diamond in the sky;
Twinkle, twinkle, little star,
How I wonder what you are.

Sleep, baby, sleep

Sleep, baby, sleep,
Your father tends the sheep,
Your mother shakes the dreamland tree,
And from it fall sweet dreams for thee,
Sleep, baby, sleep – sleep, baby, sleep.

Sleep, baby sleep,
The large stars are sheep,
The little stars are the lambs, I guess,
And the silver moon is the shepherdess,
Sleep, baby sleep – sleep, baby, sleep.

Action rhymes

Babies will respond well to the action rhymes on this page, while toddlers will enjoy joining in with those on the opposite page. You can hear the tunes for the rhymes on the opposite page, and some others, on the Usborne Quicklinks Website (see page 118).

This little piggy

(Wiggle your child's toes with each line. Start with the big toe and end with the little toe.)

    This little piggy went to market,
    This little piggy stayed at home,
    This little piggy had roast beef,
    This little piggy had none,
    This little piggy said,
    'Wee, wee, wee,' all the way home.
(Tickle your child wherever they're most ticklish.)

Round and round the garden

    Round and round the garden,
    Like a teddy bear;
(Circle your finger around your child's palm.)
    One step, two step,
(Use your fingers to 'walk' up your child's arm.)
    Tickle you under there!
(Finish by tickling them under their arms.)

This is the way the ladies ride

(Sit the baby on your knees, hold both their hands and gently bounce them in time to the rhythm of the words.)

    This is the way the ladies ride,
    Trippety-tee, trippety-tee.
    This is the way the ladies ride,
    Trippety, trippety-tee.

(You can make the bouncing a little more vigorous as the song goes on, but remember not to make any movements too vigorous with young babies.)

    This is the way the gentlemen ride,
    Gallopy-gallop, gallopy-gallop.
    This is the way the gentlemen ride,
    Gallopy-gallopy-gallop.

(For the last verse, gently sway your knees from side to side. As you reach the last line, hold the baby's hands and let them lean all the way as you say 'DOWN'.)

    This is the way the farmer rides,
    Hobble-dee-hoy, hobble-dee-hoy.
    This is the way the farmer rides,
    Hobble-dee-hoy, hobble-dee-hoy,
    ...And DOWN in the ditch!

Head, shoulders, knees and toes

(Touch your head, shoulders, knees and toes each time they are mentioned. Repeat for the second verse, but don't sing or say 'head' when you touch your head. Don't say 'head' or 'shoulders' for the third verse, and so on, until you are doing just the actions. Finish with a full run through of the words and actions.)

    Head, shoulders, knees and toes, knees and toes.
    Head, shoulders, knees and toes, knees and toes,
    And eyes, and ears and mouth and nose.
    Head, shoulders, knees and toes, knees and toes.

If you're happy and you know it

(For the first verse, clap your hands twice after the first, second and fifth lines.)

    If you're happy and you know it, clap your hands,
    If you're happy and you know it, clap your hands,
    If you're happy and you know it,
    And you really want to show it,
    If you're happy and you know it, clap your hands.

(For the second, stomp your feet twice after the first, second and fifth lines.)

    If you're happy and you know it, stomp your feet,
    If you're happy and you know it, stomp your feet,
    If you're happy and you know it,
    And you really want to show it,
    If you're happy and you know it, stomp your feet.

(On the last verse, shout 'Hoo-ray' after the first, second and fifth lines.)

    If you're happy and you know it, shout 'Hooray',
    If you're happy and you know it, shout 'Hooray',
    If you're happy and you know it,
    And you really want to show it,
    If you're happy and you know it, shout 'Hooray'.

(Other possible verses include 'pat your head' and 'jump up and down', or you can make up your own.)

Row, row, row your boat

(This action rhyme works best with two small children together. For the first verse, ask them to sit on the floor facing each other and holding hands, then show them how to row backward and forward.)

    Row, row, row your boat,
    Gently down the stream;
    Merrily, merrily, merrily, merrily,
    Life is but a dream.

(When you reach 'If you see a crocodile', ask them to jump up and make snapping jaw movements with their arms. They can SCREAM the last word.)

    Row, row, row your boat,
    Gently down the stream;
    If you see a crocodile,
    Don't forget to SCREAM!

Further help

Caring for a baby or toddler can be extremely demanding at times. It's always good to know there's help and support out there, whether it's through baby and toddler groups, local organizations or the internet.

Baby & toddler groups

Getting out and meeting other people who are taking care of babies is really worthwhile, and baby and toddler groups are the ideal place to do so. Babies get the chance to play with new toys, see different things and interact with other children – and you may meet people who are just as interested in this whole 'baby business' as you are. Some groups do lots of singing, others set up gym equipment, many just put toys out and let children play. Try to find one that gives you both what you need.

Finding groups

Most doctors' offices and many libraries will be able to tell you where groups meet. A phone call, or email, to your local parks department is also a good way of finding out what's on offer for babies and toddlers in your area. Ask your doctor if you are unsure; they can usually recommend some good groups.

Internet links

The internet is a good source of information for parents and carergivers. At the Usborne Quicklinks Website there are links to lots of websites you may find useful and other things you can download. To visit the sites, go to **www.usborne-quicklinks.com** and type the keywords 'entertain babies'.

Here are some of the things you can do via Usborne Quicklinks:

• Download a quick and easy recipe for homemade play dough.

• Print out coloring sheets, flashcards and mask templates for toddlers.

• Get tips on making simple dressing-up costumes for young children.

• Find suggestions for books suitable for babies and toddlers.

• Find advice about caring for children with specific and special needs.

Internet safety

The websites recommended in Usborne Quicklinks are regularly reviewed. However the content of a website may change at any time and Usborne Publishing is not responsible for the content or availability of websites other than its own.

What lies ahead?

If you can remember back to when the child you are caring for was a tiny newborn baby, it's easier to understand just how long a journey you have both made in the last two and a half years. Every stage of a child's development has its own particular joys and its own frustrations, and you can be very sure that the years ahead will continue to bring many more – of both!

As they approach their third year, children often start to enjoy playing with others. They are beginning to make their own friends.

Another useful book

If you have found this book useful, the next title in this series, *Entertaining and Educating Young Children,* is full of ideas for different play activities to help you through the years until a child is five years old. Just like this book, one of its main goals is to reassure you that, whenever children are playing and having fun, they are learning, too.

More about development

The following four pages give you more detail about how babies develop, and what they will probably be able to do at certain ages. Keep in mind, though, that these are only guidelines, and try not to worry if a child is later, or earlier, doing something than is suggested here. Baby and childcare experts emphasize that all children are different, develop at their own rate, and have their own likes and dislikes, just as adults do. Very few of them will do everything exactly when it is shown here.

What to look for

The information on the following pages covers baby and toddler development from birth up to the age of two and a half in these four areas:

Movement skills
This is about what babies' and toddlers' bodies can do.

Hand-eye coordination
This covers what they can do with their hands and fingers.

Language development
This is about what they can hear, say and understand.

Emotional and social development
This is about how they relate to caregivers and other children.

0–1 month (from birth)

Movement: can turn head to the side slightly, particularly toward soft light, when lying on their back or front. Reflex stepping if held under armpits. 'Rooting' for milk. Head heavy and lolling.

Hand-eye coordination: reflex gripping of a finger with their fingers. Hands usually in a fist. Limited vision – can only see things about 10 inches away.

Language: cries for attention, and can already have different cries for different needs. Startled by loud noises – flails in the Moro reflex.

Emotional development: can be soothed by soft voices and by rocking motion. May respond to smiles and recognize their mother's face by becoming still.

2–3 months

Movement: can turn to both sides more easily and lifts head if laid on tummy. Thrashes arms and kicks legs vigorously if excited.

Hand-eye coordination: fascination with own fingers and hands, which are now open. Follows an object with the eyes, and may reach out toward it and swipe at it as their vision improves. Can hold a rattle for a few moments.

Language: makes several distinct cooing and gurgling sounds. May chuckle or laugh at a soft 'Boo!'. Quietens when hears background noise and may turn toward it.

Emotional development: responds to familiar voices, especially to singing and music. May recognize familiar sounds, such as bath water running. Smiles at caregivers' faces. Shows emotions with facial expressions more.

3–6 months

Movement: enjoys rolling, and will probably roll all the way over. Can hold head up. Tries to lift head when trying to sit, and props up body on arms when lying on tummy. Pushes legs against crib or floor, and against your lap if standing upright. Can sit upright with support.

Hand-eye coordination: focus on wanting to touch things, and hold them. Touches or holds breast or bottle during feeding. Can see most objects at any distance. Holds objects and puts most into their mouths to find out about them.

Language: makes sounds to attract attention. More sustained babbling, with strings of 'bah' and 'dah' sounds. May have 'conversations' with others, taking turns in producing sounds.

Emotional development: recognizes familiar faces and situations and responds to them. Copies facial expressions more accurately. Predicts exciting parts of rhymes and songs.

6–9 months

Movement: rolls from back to front easily. Can sit upright without support. May start crawling, climbing stairs, and pulling themselves upright using furniture.

Hand-eye coordination: can pick things up, develops a 'pincer' grip, using the thumb and forefinger by nine months. Able to hold and play with smaller, detailed objects such as pop-together or pull-apart toys.

Language: uses more consonants to make sounds like 'ma' and 'pa' and longer sounds, such as 'nananana'. Listens when others are talking around them.

Emotional development: waves 'bye-bye' and responds to own name. Shows distinct emotions, such as anger, and may get upset if you are. Actively participates in games involving hiding and revealing, such as 'peekaboo'. Starts eating solid food.

9–12 months

Movement: crawls rapidly, cruises around the room, holding hands or furniture. May be able to stand supported for a short time and take some steps, if holding your hand. Great interest, and more success, in climbing stairs. Able to sit down from standing.

Hand-eye coordination: enjoys games involving coordination, such as give and take games and 'pat-a-cake'. Has mastered pincer grip. Can fit shapes into slots in simple shape-sorter toys. Interest in interactive toys, with buttons or strings to pull.

Language: first words said during these months, which are usually their names for familiar people or things. Much more varied intonation in their speech sounds.

Emotional development: wants to explore and find out about things. Interest in filling and emptying. Able to understand simple phrases such as 'no' and 'all gone'.

12–18 months

Movement: starts walking, with increasing steadiness. Can change direction while walking and bend to pick things up. Crawls up stairs and can kneel upright. Can throw things.

Hand-eye coordination: can hold an object in each hand and bring them together, such as a peg and hammer toy. Pushes and pulls toys. Begins to feed self. Can make marks on paper with a crayon. Enjoys inset puzzles. Points to objects with index finger.

Language: uses several words, but knows and understands many more. Enjoys books, songs and rhymes and may try to sing their tunes. Learning new words all the time.

Emotional development: increasingly strong-willed, with definite likes and dislikes. Very focused on main caregiver, enjoys copying their actions – and often distressed if separated from them.

18–24 months

Movement: can run, ride on toys, clamber over things, walk upstairs if holding a hand, is generally very active and interested in exploring.

Hand-eye coordination: interested in knobs, zippers and screw lids. Can build a tower of several blocks, and do simple jigsaw puzzles. Matches two objects together. Enjoys playing with dough, water and with balls, though not always successful in catching them yet. Enjoys art activities, such as painting and drawing, and can produce scribbles back and forth.

Language: vocabulary expands rapidly during these months. Enjoys hearing language, particularly in one-to-one conversation and in stories. By two, probably saying two-word sentences such as 'Milk gone'.

Emotional development: recognizes familiar faces in photographs and recognizes characters in picture books. Aware of other children, though still plays alone. May be interested in using a potty.

2–2½ years

Movement: can jump off a step, or off the ground. Can carry something, such as a ball, while running. Can make push-along toys move. Increasingly physically coordinated and confident.

Hand-eye coordination: preference for right- or left-handedness becomes obvious around now. More control of paintbrushes or crayons, and can thread large beads onto string and mold with play dough. Enjoys sorting toys into groups, or families and playing alone. Ball control improving rapidly.

Language: speaks more in two- or even three-word sentences. Can name body parts, familiar people and colors. 'Talks' to toys and enjoys hearing stories. Very curious, asking lots of questions.

Emotional development: starts pretend play, acting simple roles. Growing understanding of household rituals, such as washing hands, sitting at table, using silverware and dressing and undressing. Begins to be aware of others' feelings and needs.

Index

Acknowledgements

For Bethan, Rhiannon and Mari Young with love from Mum.

With thanks to...

Baby Chloe, Baby Milly, Finley, Tulsa Area Safe Kids Organization, and all the staff, parents and children at Cannons Health Club Nursery, Surbiton, UK, for their kind help and support of Shelagh McNicholas (and for being superb models).

Photo credits:

The publishers are grateful to the following for permission to reproduce material:
p9 © Mother & Baby Picture Library/Ian Hooton; p10 © TEK IMAGE/SCIENCE PHOTO LIBRARY; p18 © Mother & Baby Picture Library/Ruth Jenkinson; p19 © Mother & Baby Picture Library/Ruth Jenkinson; p27 © Mother & Baby Picture Library/Ruth Jenkinson; p29 © Mother & Baby Picture Library/Paul Mitchell; p33 © Getty Images/Anne Ackermann; p41 © Comstock Images /Alamy; p43 © Comstock Images/Alamy; p51 © Dynamic Graphics Group/Creatas/ Alamy; p52 © IAN BODDY/SCIENCE PHOTO LIBRARY; p55 © Getty Images/Dag Sundberg; p60 © Elizabeth Hathon/CORBIS; p68 © Getty Images/Digital Vision; p73 © David Pollack/CORBIS; p93 © SAS/Alamy; p96 © Jennie Woodcock; Reflections Photolibrary/CORBIS; p100 © Piotr Kapa/CORBIS; p105 © Royalty-Free/CORBIS; p106 © Picture Partners/Alamy; p110 LAUREN SHEAR/SCIENCE PHOTO LIBRARY

Additonal picture research: Claire Masset, Emma Helbrough and Ruth King

Additional consultants: Alison Bell (swimming), Emma Sheppard, St. John Ambulance (first aid) and Wendy Scrase (exercise)

Additional illustrations: Dubravka Kolanovic

Digital imaging: Keith Furnival